*Pocket*
# KUALA LUMPUR

TOP SIGHTS • LOCAL LIFE • MADE EASY

**Robert Kelly**

# In This Book

## QuickStart Guide

Your keys to understanding the city — we help you decide what to do and how to do it

**Need to Know**
Tips for a smooth trip

**Neighbourhoods**
What's where

## Explore Kuala Lumpur

The best things to see and do, neighbourhood by neighbourhood

**Top Sights**
Make the most of your visit

**Local Life**
The insider's city

## The Best of Kuala Lumpur

The city's highlights in handy lists to help you plan

**Best Walks**
See the city on foot

**Kuala Lumpur's Best...**
The best experiences

## Survival Guide

Tips and tricks for a seamless, hassle-free city experience

**Getting Around**
Travel like a local

**Essential Information**
Including where to stay

Our selection of the city's best places to eat, drink and experience:

◉ **Sights**

✖ **Eating**

🚇 **Drinking**

✦ **Entertainment**

🔒 **Shopping**

These symbols give you the vital information for each listing:

| | |
|---|---|
| ☏ Telephone Numbers | 👪 Family-Friendly |
| ⏱ Opening Hours | 🐾 Pet-Friendly |
| ℗ Parking | 🚌 Bus |
| 🚭 Nonsmoking | ⛴ Ferry |
| @ Internet Access | Ⓜ Metro |
| 📶 Wi-Fi Access | Ⓢ Subway |
| 🥗 Vegetarian Selection | 🚋 Tram |
| 📖 English-Language Menu | 🚆 Train |

Find each listing quickly on maps for each neighbourhood:

### Bar Hemingway

16 🚇 Map p233, B2

Legend has it that Hemi
self, wielding a machine
~~rate this timber-pan
~~tered bar during
showpiece is a
~~en by Papa ar
town. Dress
s.com; Hôtel Rit
; ⏱6.30pm-2a

# Lonely Planet's Kuala Lumpur

Lonely Planet Pocket Guides are designed to get you straight to the heart of the city.

Inside you'll find all the must-see sights, plus tips to make your visit to each one really memorable. We've split the city into easy-to-navigate neighbourhoods and provided clear maps so you'll find your way around with ease. Our expert authors have searched out the best of the city: walks, food, nightlife and shopping, to name a few. Because you want to explore, our 'Local Life' pages will take you to some of the most exciting areas to experience the real Kuala Lumpur.

And of course you'll find all the practical tips you need for a smooth trip: itineraries for short visits, how to get around, and how much to tip the guy who serves you a drink at the end of a long day's exploration.

It's your guarantee of a really great experience.

## Our Promise

You can trust our travel infor-mation because Lonely Planet authors visit the places we write about, each and every edition. We never accept freebies for positive coverage, so you can rely on us to tell it like it is.

## QuickStart Guide 7

Kuala Lumpur
Top Sights ........................ 8

Kuala Lumpur
Local Life ......................... 12

Kuala Lumpur
Day Planner ..................... 14

Need to Know .................. 16

Kuala Lumpur
Neighbourhoods .............. 18

## Explore Kuala Lumpur 21

**22**    Golden Triangle

**40**    Petronas Towers & KLCC

**60**    Chinatown & Merdeka Square

**80**    Masjid India, Chow Kit & Kampung Baru

**98**    Lake Gardens & Brickfields

### Worth a Trip:

Pudu .................................................. 38

Ampang Amble ................................. 92

Batu Caves ....................................... 94

Forestry Research Institute
of Malaysia (FRIM) ......................... 96

Thean Hou Temple .......................... 118

Boutique-Hopping in
Bangsar Baru ................................... 120

# The Best of Kuala Lumpur  123

## Kuala Lumpur's Best Walks

A Stroll Through Kampung Baru ..... **124**

Chinatown Architecture Ramble ...... **126**

## Kuala Lumpur's Best...

Street Food & Food Courts ..................... **128**

Bars & Cafes .................................. **130**

Shopping ....................................... **132**

With Kids ....................................... **134**

For Free ........................................ **135**

Clubs & Entertainment ..................... **136**

Religious & Heritage Buildings ........... **138**

Green Spaces .................................. **139**

Museums & Galleries ........................ **140**

Spas & Wellness ............................. **142**

# Survival Guide  143

Before You Go ................... **144**

Arriving in
Kuala Lumpur ................... **145**

Getting Around ................. **146**

Essential Information ....... **148**

Language ......................... **152**

# QuickStart Guide

Kuala Lumpur Top Sights ............................. 8

Kuala Lumpur Local Life ........................... 12

Kuala Lumpur Day Planner ..................... 14

Need to Know ............................................ 16

Kuala Lumpur Neighbourhoods ............................ 18

## Welcome to Kuala Lumpur

Glitzy malls rub shoulders with street markets, gleaming skyscrapers loom over colonial buildings, and world-class restaurants vie for patronage with bustling open-air satay stands: Kuala Lumpur may be racing toward the future, but its rich cultural heritage refuses to be left behind. From steaming bowls of *asam laksa* to sinfully sweet morsels of *kueh*, the very best part is its legendary food.

Petaling Street Market (p79)
LAURIE NOBLE/GETTY IMAGES ©

# ◉ Kuala Lumpur
## Top Sights

### Petronas Towers (p42)

It's impossible to resist the magnetic allure of these 452m-high structures, embodiment of Malaysia's transformation into a modern nation. The views both from and of the towers are equally riveting.

## Tun Abdul Razak Heritage Park (p100)

Better known as the Lake Gardens, this is KL's major green space, with a day's worth of sights including botanical gardens, a bird park and a host of surrounding museums and colonial architecture.

### Merdeka Square (p62)

There is nowhere better in KL to soak up its British colonial past, including its Mughal-inspired architecture, than around this former cricket green which first saw the raising of the Malaysian flag in 1957.

### Islamic Arts Museum (p102)

This terrific museum highlights the diversity of art – from miniature painting to interior design – and the richness of regional variation in the Islamic world: from the Middle East, through China, India and Southeast Asia.

### Batu Caves (p94)

In these soaring limestone caves – the country's top Hindu pilgrimage site – intricate geological formations compete for your attention with colourful shrines and psychedelic dioramas.

### Menara KL (p44)

Rival to the Petronas Towers for glorious city views, this 421m-high telecommunications tower is best approached through the jungle trails (and canopy walk) of Bukit Nanas.

LAURIE NOBLE/GETTY IMAGES ©

### Forestry Research Institute of Malaysia (FRIM)
(p96)

A natural escape from KL's urban grind, this 600-hectare forest reserve sports hiking trails, a 200m-long canopy walkway and quiet lanes for leisurely biking.

### Royal Museum
(p104)

The home of Malaysia's king until 2011, this grand sprawling mansion was built in 1928 by a Chinese tin tycoon to house his numerous children (and wives).

### Thean Hou Temple
(p118)

The glorious sunsets over the city, and the devotional atmosphere during Chinese festival times, draw visitors to this massive, fantastically gaudy Chinese temple atop Robson Hill.

WEWEK/GETTY IMAGES ©

# Kuala Lumpur
## Local Life

*Insider tips to help you find the real city*

Getting local in KL's diverse neighborhoods isn't just about tucking into hawker food under the gaze of the Petronas Towers (though this is great fun, by the way). Almost everyone can find their tribe in this city, from mall rats to old-school foodies, street photographers and aficionados of third-wave coffee.

### Ampang Amble (p92)

▶ Leafy neighbourhoods
▶ Food

This diverse neighbourhood of ethnic villages bumping up against whitewashed embassies boasts a number of treats. You can stroll KL's loveliest tree-lined lanes with early-morning joggers, make batik in an outdoor workshop, and, in season (if you're very game), try an all-you-can-eat durian feast.

### Pudu (p38)

▶ Street food
▶ Urban exploration

Hankering for the flavours of Chinatown without the crowds? Visit this laid-back Chinese neighbourhood, with some of KL's most charming pockets of shophouses and crowd-pleasing street eats. The sprawling Pudu wet market is the city's largest.

### A Taste of the Golden Triangle (p24)

▶ Street food
▶ Bars

More than anything else, the search for the next great meal makes this city tick. Street food is everyone's obsession, but in this area of town you can also observe how the experience has been moved indoors without compromising on atmosphere (much).

### Boutique-Hopping in Bangsar Baru (p120)

▶ Shopping
▶ Restaurants

Come for the shopping, stay for the food. Or do the reverse in this buzzing suburban enclave brimming with trendy cafes, a diverse selection of restaurants, and cool boutiques run by up-and-coming local designers.

Little India (p115)

Food stall in Bangsar Baru (p120)

**Other great places to experience the city like a local:**

Multicultural Markets (p88)

Coffee Stain by Joseph (p36)

Chetty Street (p68)

KL Academy of Traditional Chinese Medicine (p78)

Chin Woo Stadium (p76)

Sri Sakthi Vinayagar Temple (p108)

Little India's Street Food (p115)

Buddhist Maha Vihara (p110)

KEVIN LANG/ALAMY ©

# Kuala Lumpur
## Day Planner

## Day One

Begin at **Merdeka Square** (p62) to see where the Malaysian flag was first raised in 1957. Eclectic colonial architecture surrounds the square, from the Mughal-inspired **Masjid Jamek** (p66) and **Sultan Abdul Samad Building** (p63) to the Tudor-style **Royal Selangor Club** (p63). The **KL City Gallery** (p63) provides a great insight into the city's history and architecture.

Head to Chinatown for lunch: good choices include **Peter Hoe Beyond Cafe** (p126), **Old China Café** (p72) or **LOKL** (p73). If you need a caffeine boost, **Moontree House** (p74) is around the corner from the Old China Café. Stay on to explore the neighbourhood's temples and heritage shophouses, as well as the **Central Market** (p67), with its excellent souvenir and antique shopping, and knockout **Museum of Ethnic Arts** (p68). A *roti canai* at the adjacent **Restoran Yusoof dan Zakhir** (p71) will revive flagging spirits.

In the evening visit the **Petronas Towers** (p42; (pre-book online) for mesmerising sunset views. Afterwards stroll **KLCC Park** (p43) and see the towers gleam against the night sky, then finish on a high at the **Troika** (p53) complex for dinner, drinks and even more killer views.

## Day Two

Start with a morning stroll in **Tun Abdul Razak Heritage Park** (p100), the city's largest green oasis. Spend some time with hornbills at the wonderful **KL Bird Park** (FRIM; p101), then smell the flowers at the **Botanical Garden** (p101).

Lunch at the **Hornbill Restaurant** (p113), or head down to the **Colonial Cafe** (p115), located in the handsome Majestic Hotel, with its menu of Hainanese cuisine beloved by KL's colonial rulers. After lunch, marvel at the **Old KL Train Station** (p108) and **Masjid Negara** (p110), the national mosque, before hitting the museums, including the must-see **Islamic Arts Museum** (p102) and the **National Museum** (p108 – the walk between the two is lovely along Lake Perdana – as well as the quirky **Royal Malaysia Police Museum** (p101).

For dinner take a taxi to hip Jln Mesui or Changkit Bukit Bintang for fine Malay cuisine at **Bijan** (p30) or more homely Nonya fare at **Lima Blas** (p29). There's no need to travel afterwards for fun: there are plenty of bars, clubs and live-music venues in the surrounding streets, such as **Taps Beer Bar** (p31) and **Frangipani** (p31).

**Short on time?**

We've arranged Kuala Lumpur 's must-sees into these day-by-day itineraries to make sure you see the very best of the city in the time you have available.

## Day Three

☀ Try a traditional breakfast at **Imbi Market** (p24, then grab some snacks for the road and take the train or taxi to the **Forestry Research Institute of Malaysia** (p97). Explore the enchanting woods (perhaps by bike), see traditional wooden houses and take the canopy walkway high above the jungle floor.

☀ Next stop: **Batu Caves** (p95). Nosh on veggie dosa at **Rani Vilas Restoran** (p95) when you arrive, then climb the 272 stairs to the Main Cave, take the Dark Cave tour, and explore the surrealistic Ramayana Cave. Head back to the city via **Lake Titiwangsa** (p85) for postcard-perfect pics of KL, then pop into the **National Visual Arts Gallery** (p85) for a lesson in contemporary Malaysian art.

☾ For dinner head to Sentul West (p137) and wander the very photogenic old railway depot. Dine by candlelight at the lake and perhaps take in a show at the **Kuala Lumpur Performing Arts Centre** (p137). Still got some energy left? Move on to **Zouk** (p55) to dance the night away.

## Day Four

☀ After breakfast in Chinatown, head to the sprawling **Royal Museum** (p119), the Malaysian king's former home. Then take a taxi to Brickfields, passing through KL's largest Chinese cemetery. In Brickfields visit the **Hindu temples** (p110); check their Facebook pages, including www.facebook.com/SriKandaswamyTemple, to see if any festivals are happening.

☀ Fuel up on tandoori chicken and the city's best dhal *makhani* at **Jassal Tandoori Restaurant** (p113) before walking up Bukit Nanas through the **KL Forest Eco Park** (p45) to **Menara KL** (p44). Then stroll down to Bukit Bintang and pop into upscale food courts **Lot 10 Hutong** (p25) for a street-food snack... indoors. If you need it, or simply want it, indulge in a massage at **Donna Spa** (p28) on Starhill Gallery's Pamper Floor.

☾ Plan on eating outdoors tonight. If it's a Tuesday, Thursday or Sunday, consider joining a walking tour of **Kampung Baru** (p84), a village in the heart of the city; there are plenty of good dinner options here. Otherwise, go for Chinese at **Hakka** (p29); Chinese, Malay and Thai on **Jalan Alor** (p25); or hawkers' specialities at **Keong Kee** (p39).

# Need to Know

**For more information,
see Survival Guide (p143)**

### Currency
Malaysian Ringgit (RM)

### Language
English
Bahasa Malaysia

### Visas
Generally not required for stays up to
90 days.

### Money
ATMs widely available, but complex local
rules sometimes impose low daily limits
or reject foreign cards. Credit cards widely
accepted in shops, hotels and midrange
and top-end restaurants.

### Mobile Phones
Malaysia is on a GSM and 3G and 4G
network. Local SIM cards work on most
phones and can be purchased at the airport

### Time
MYT (Malaysia Time; UTC/GMT plus
eight hours)

### Plugs & Adaptors
Plugs have three square pins; electrical
current is 220/230V. Most visitors will require
an adaptor and possibly a transformer.

### Tipping
Small change on bill often left at restaurants.
Tipping for extra service from hotel porters and
taxi drivers is common and appreciated.

## ① Before You Go

## Your Daily Budget

### Budget less than RM150
- ► Dorm beds RM30–45
- ► Hawker stalls or food courts RM6–12
- ► Visit one pricier big sight every two days

### Midrange RM150-400
- ► Double room in boutique hotel RM120–200
- ► Visit sights by tour bus to avoid taxi hassles
- ► Meal with two beers at local restaurants
RM40–60

### Top End more than RM400
- ► Double room at colonial mansion from RM600
- ► Fine dining on ethnic or Western cuisine
RM350 plus

## Useful Websites

**Lonely Planet** (www.lonelyplanet.com/
kuala-lumpur) Destination information, hotel
booking, traveller forum and more.

**Visit KL** (www.klcitygallery.com) Good tourist
authority website.

**TimeOut Kuala Lumpur** (www.timeout.com/
kuala-lumpur) Excellent insider coverage of
local life, attractions, restaurants and bars.

**Malaysian Insider** (www.themalaysianin-
sider.com) A non-censored online-only news
outlet for the scoop on politics and culture.

## Advance Planning

**Three months before** Book hotel if coming
in summer months or during one of the
many public holidays.

**One month before** Check Pusaka (www.
facebook.com/pages/Pusaka) and tourism
and temple websites for festivals.

**One week before** Book a ticket online for
the Petronas Towers, and make reservations
for top-end restaurants or bars.

## ② Arriving in Kuala Lumpur

Most international visitors arrive at Kuala Lumpur International Airport (www.klia.com.my), the city's primary air transport hub. There are two terminals: KLIA II is the low-cost carrier terminal (such as for Air Asia). The airport is about 50km south of the city centre.

### ✈ From Kuala Lumpur International Airport (KLIA)

| Destination | Best Transport |
| --- | --- |
| KL Sentral | KLIA Ekspres, airport express bus |
| Chinatown | KLIA Ekspres (then transfer to LRT), airport bus to Puduraya |
| KLCC | KLIA Ekspres (then transfer to LRT), taxi |

### ✈ At the Airport

**Kuala Lumpur International Airport** Both KLIA I and II have ATMs and moneychanging facilities and loads of shops and restaurants. After immigration there are duty-free stores, telecom shops where you can purchase local SIM cards, and stands for purchasing taxi, train and bus coupons. Note some buses run to city hotels before their final destination at KL Sentral. Also be aware that the walk through KLIA II to immigration is exceptionally long; make use of the shuttle cars if needed.

## ③ Getting Around

KL's public transport can usually get you to the general area you want to go. From there walking or taking a taxi is best. The tourist buses are also very handy.

### 🚌 Tourist Bus

KL Hop-On Hop-Off buses (www.myhoponhopoff.com) stop at all major attractions, malls and hotels in the city. Buses run frequently, and day and multiday passes are available. The buses are one of the most popular, hassle-free ways to see the sights, though between 4pm and 6pm they are very crowded.

### 🚈 LRT, Komuter Train & Monorail

Together these three systems form a decent network for getting around the city, though they aren't well integrated at the stations they share. The monorail (www.myrapid.com.my) runs through the heart of the city and connects many of the top tourist sites and areas. The LRT (Light Rapid Transit; www.my-rapid.com.my), KL's metro, is good for trips into the suburbs, while the KTM Komuter Train (www.ktmkomuter.com.my) will whisk you out to Batu Caves and close to FRIM.

### 🚕 Taxi

Taxis are cheap and ubiquitous except when it rains. However, drivers have a bad reputation and in tourist areas overcharging is rife: use a taxi booking smartphone app such as MyTeksi. Most shopping malls also have a taxi stand for safe hassle-free bookings.

# Kuala Lumpur
## Neighbourhoods

**Masjid India, Chow Kit & Kampung Baru (p80)**
These distinct ethnic neighborhoods attract with lively markets, and a *kampung* (village) in the heart of the city.

**Worth a Trip**

👁 **Top Sights**

Forestry Research Institute of Malaysia (FRIM)

Batu Caves

Thean Hou Temple

*Tun Abdul Razak Heritage Park* 👁

*Merdeka Square* 👁

*Islamic Arts Museum* 👁

*Royal Museum* 👁

**Lake Gardens & Brickfields (p98)**
The city's green lungs are surrounded by top museums, while south is KL's official Little India.

👁 **Top Sights**

Tun Abdul Razak Heritage Park

Royal Museum

Islamic Arts Museum

**Petronas Towers & KLCC (p40)**
This is where KL shows off its eclectic urban accomplishments, from skyscrapers boasting chic bars, to towers atop pristine jungle.

**◉ Top Sights**

Petronas Towers

Menara KL

*Petronas Towers*
◉

*Menara KL*
◉

**Golden Triangle (p22)**
The Golden Triangle may seem like one large shopping mall, but go west for eat streets, hip bars and clusters of small restaurants.

**Chinatown & Merdeka Square (p60)**
Historical architecture, from Moghul mosques to colonial mansions, and Chinese and Indian cuisine, make this KL's most popular tourist area.

**◉ Top Sights**

Merdeka Square

## Explore
# Kuala Lumpur

Golden Triangle ............................. | 22

Petronas Towers & KLCC ............. | 40

Chinatown & Merdeka Square .... | 60

Masjid India, Chow Kit &
Kampung Baru ............................. | 80

Lake Gardens & Brickfields ......... | 98

**Worth a Trip**

Pudu .................................................. 38
Ampang Amble .............................. 92
Batu Caves ...................................... 94
Forestry Research Institute
of Malaysia (FRIM) ...................... 96
Thean Hou Temple ....................... 118
Boutique-Hopping in
Bangsar Baru .............................. 120

Sri Mahamariamman Temple (p66)
MIXA/GETTY IMAGES ©

Explore

# Golden Triangle

The financial and commercial heart of KL is not just high rises, shopping malls and construction sites. There's plenty of street life – and, most importantly, street eating – and as you head west, small and personalised venues take over. The alfresco dining on Jln Alor and the frenetic bar scene on Changkit Bukit Bintang – and its hipper cousin Jln Mesui – attract big crowds nightly.

# The Sights in a Day

 Begin with a swing through **Imbi Market** (p24), snacking and snapping pics to your heart's content. If you wake late then the specialty coffees and sandwiches at **Feeka** (p29) will get you going. Afterwards, grab a taxi to Bukit Bintang. Start at **Starhill Culinary Studio** (p28), with a class on local cooking, followed by an indulgence at **Donna Spa** (p28) or tea at **Luk Yu** (p34).

For lunch move down the block to the indoor hawker paradise at **Lot 10 Hutong** (p25). If you are in the mood for shopping, there's youth fashion at **Fahrenheit88** (p36), endless electronics at **Plaza Low Yat** (p37), and a wide selection of local and international brands at **Pavilion KL** (p36). At **Royal Selangor** (p36) browse the gorgeous pewterware and learn some city history.

Now head west and begin your evening with tapas and a beer at **Pisco Bar** (p31). Move on to dinner at **Lima Blas** (p29) or nearby **Frangipani** (p31). Afterwards, look for live music at **No Black Tie** (p35), craft beers at **Taps Beer Bar** (p31), or a rowdy good time at one of the many drinking venues along Changkat Bukit Bintang.

To feast like a local in the Golden Triangle, see p24.

## Local Life
A Taste of the Golden Triangle (p24)

 **Best of Kuala Lumpur**

**Clubs & Entertainment**
No Black Tie (p35)
Blueboy Discotheque (p34)
Frangipani (p31)

**Bars & Cafes**
Pisco Bar (p31)
Taps Beer Bar (p31)
Feeka Coffee Roasters (p29)
Green Man (p34)
Frangipani (p31)

**Street Food & Food Courts**
Jalan Alor (p25)
Lot 10 Hutong (p25)

**Spas & Wellness**
Kenko (p28)
Donna Spa (p28)

## Getting There

**Monorail** Bukit Bintang station is in the heart of the district.

**Bus** KL Hop-On Hop-Off buses link the Golden Triangle with other tourist areas and sights in KL.

**Walking** The area is compact and easy to walk from one end to the other.

# Local Life
# A Taste of the Golden Triangle

Street food is everywhere in the Golden Triangle, though in KL locals accept it neither has to be prepared nor consumed outdoors. Given the city's obsession with malls and air-conditioning, many hawker stalls have moved indoors, though if you want it old-school this area still shines.

**❶ Breakfast at Imbi Market**
Breakfast is a cheerful affair in the courtyard of this walled traditional **market** (Pasar Baru Bukit Bintang; Jln Kampung; dishes RM5-10; ⏱6.30am-12.30pm Tue-Sun; taxi). Time-tested stalls include **Sisters Crispy Popiah** for wraps; **Teluk Intan Chee Cheung Fun** for oyster-and-peanut congee and egg pudding; and **Ah Weng Koh Hainan Tea** for coffee or tea (or both together in its special drink).

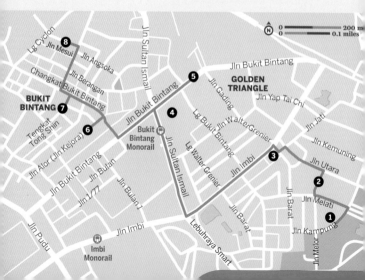

### ❷ Jalan Melati & Jalan Utara

Walk around **Jln Melati** and **Jln Utara** for glimpses into the casual outdoor life that still dominates even in neighbourhoods bordering KL's newly developing financial district. Where there's a spreading tree it seems you'll find a food stall, a few plastic chairs and happy relaxed customers. These streets also have pre-war houses to admire.

### ❸ Restoran Win Heng Seng

Often hawkers congregate in a single streetside food court such as at **Restoran Win Heng Seng** (183 Jln Imbi; dishes RM5-10), which rivals Imbi Market as a popular place for a local breakfast. Try the pork ball noodles or the *char kway teow* (fried noodles in a dark soy sauce).

### ❹ Lot 10 Hutong

**Lot 10 Hutong** (Basement, Lot 10, 50 Jln Sultan Ismail; dishes RM9-18; ⏱10am-10pm; monorail Bukit Bintang) was the first KL mall to encourage top hawkers to open branches in a basement food court. The well-designed space has pulled in names such as **Soong Kee**, which has served beef noodles since 1945. Look also for oyster omelettes at **Kong Tai**, Cantonese porridge at **Hon Kee**, and Hokkien mee at **Kim Lian Kee**.

### ❺ Bintang Walk

This short strip of prime real estate is tops for people-watching. **Al-Amar Express** (www.al-amar.com; 179 Jln Bukit Bintang; dishes RM8-25; ⏱8am-3am; monorail Bukit Bintang), a glass-encased

streetside restaurant, is a great place to take it all in with a Turkish coffee.

### ❻ Jalan Alor

KL's biggest collection of roadside restaurants sprawls along **Jalan Alor** (⏱5pm-late; monorail to Bukit Bintang). From around 5pm till late every evening, the street transforms into a continuous open-air venue. Most places serve alcohol and you can sample pretty much every Malay-Chinese dish imaginable. In the afternoon you can pick up a fortifying fresh coconut or sugarcane drink and watch the preparation for the nightly feast.

### ❼ Tengkat Tong Shin

Here's another short street loaded with restaurants and hawker stalls. Among the most celebrated is the nothing-to-look-at **Ngau Kee** (Tengkat Tong Shin; noodles RM8-9; ⏱5pm-4am; monorail Bukit Bintang) at the end of the street, which serves a variety of beef noodle soups. If you aren't hungry, Tengkat Tong Shin's art deco and eclectic-style pre-war shophouses are worth a look-in.

### ❽ Changkat Bukit Bintang & Jalan Mesui

The last two blocks of **Changkat Bukit Bintang** support a growing number of bars that offer everything from a lounge for contemplating single malt whisky to a corner den for cheap draught and pub quizzes. Around the corner, the cafes and bars on **Jalan Mesui** cater to a younger local crowd.

A  B  C  D

KL Forest
Eco Park

1

Jln Raja Chulan

Changkat Raja Chulan

2

12

9

Jln Ceylon

Lg Cyclon

Jln Mesui

Jln Berangan

2 20

4 11

BUKIT
BINTANG

16

17

13

Jln Nagansari

Jln Angsoka

Jln Bedara

Jln Beremj

10

Changkat Bukit Bintang

Jln Sahabat

3

Tengkat Tong Shin

4

5

Jln Tong Shin

Jln Pudu

Jln Alor (Jln Kejora)

8

Jln Bukit Bintang

Jln Bulan

Jln Bulan 1

Jln 1/77

26

5

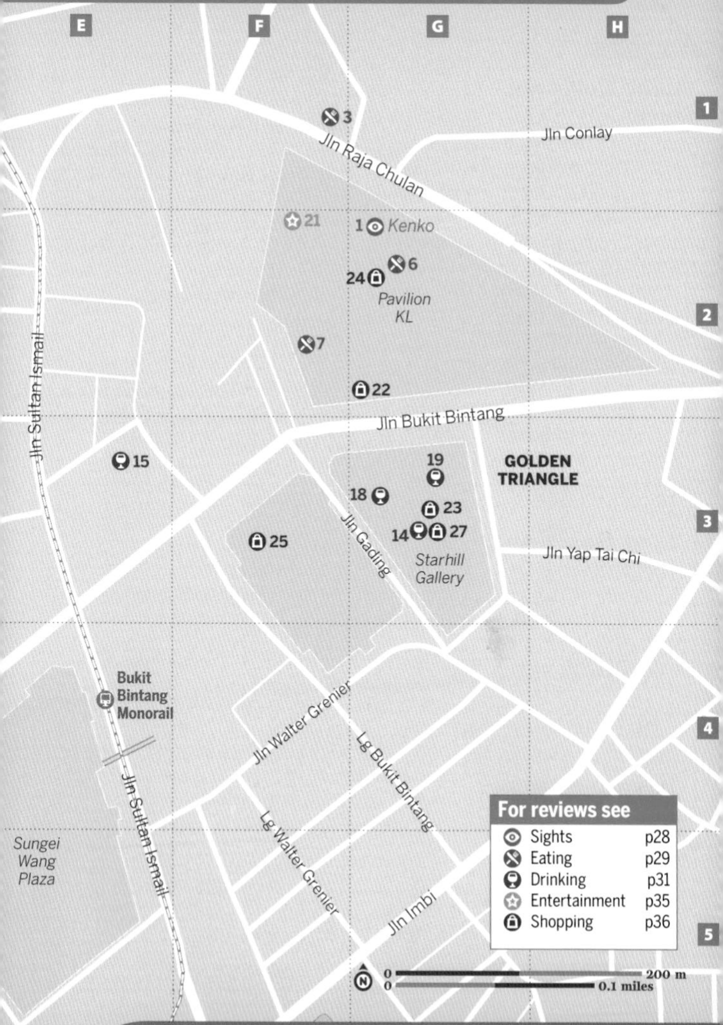
E
F
G
H
1
2
3
4
5
3
Jln Conlay
Jln Raja Chulan
21
1 Kenko
6
24
Pavilion KL
7
22
Jln Bukit Bintang
Jln Sultan Ismail
15
19
GOLDEN TRIANGLE
18
23
14
27
25
Jln Gading
Starhill Gallery
Jln Yap Tai Chi
Bukit Bintang Monorail
Jln Walter Grenier
Lg Bukit Bintang
Jln Sultan Ismail
Lg Walter Grenier
Sungei Wang Plaza
Jln Imbi
For reviews see
Sights p28
Eating p29
Drinking p31
Entertainment p35
Shopping p36
N
0 200 m
0 0.1 miles

# Sights

## Starhill Culinary Studio
COOKING COURSE

Sign up for a two- to three-hour class and you'll not only get top instruction in this well-designed culinary art studio, but you'll also be well fed. Classes are held at the Starhill Gallery (see 23 🔒 Map p26, G3), vary daily and include Malay and Nonya dishes, Japanese cuisine, and Asian and Western desserts. Private classes can also be arranged.
(📞2782 3810; www.starhillculinarystudio. com; Muse Floor, Starhill Gallery, 181 Jln Bukit Bintang; public classes RM68-258; ⏰9am-6pm Tue-Sun; monorail Bukit Bintang)

## Kenko
SPA

1 ◉ Map p26, G2

This popular branch of the Singapore-based reflexology and massage chain offers a variety of massage therapies. Its popular and very hygienic fish spa starts at RM38 should you wish skin to be nibbled off your tootsies.
(📞2141 6651; www.kenko.com.sg; Level 5, Pavilion KL, 169 Jln Bukit Bintang; ⏰10am-10pm; monorail Bukit Bintang)

## Donna Spa
SPA

This Balinese-style spa is one of the most popular on the Pamper Floor of the Starhill Gallery (see 23 🔒 Map p26, G3). Massages start at RM200.

---

### Understand

## What's in a Name?

The Golden Triangle is one of the most expensive swathes of real estate in the city, and is bordered by Jln Ampang, Jln Imbi/Pudu and Jln Tun Razak, which form a triangle.

And those street names? Well, Ampang means 'dam' and refers to the tin mining that made KL rich. Tun Razak was the second prime minister, while Pudu means 'half in the jungle', a reference to its early location.

Most road names in this part of town, however, were changed post-independence. In fact over 500 names were changed from 1980 to 2008, and in 2014 another eight were changed. Jln Alor, the famous food street, is actually officially Jln Kejora, but next to no one uses that.

**Sultan Ismail** – after the Sultan of Johor

**Jln P Ramlee** – after Malaysia's most beloved actor

**Bukit Bintang** – literally 'star hill'

**Jln Raja Chulan** – after a member of the Perak royal family

**Jln Tunku Abdul Rahman** – after Malaysia's first prime minister

(☎2141 8999; www.donnaspa.net; Pamper Floor, Starhill Gallery, 181 Jln Bukit Bintang; ⏱10am-midnight; monorail Bukit Bintang)

# Eating

### Lima Blas
CHINESE $$

2  Map p26, C2

Set in an old shophouse with a bric-a-brac design that channels old Malaysia, this is a top spot for a casual night out of exotic food. Try the Nonya fried chicken, eggplant in sambal sauce and the *sago gula melaka* (sago pearls in a brown sugar sauce). (☎2110 1289; www.facebook.com/pages/Lima-Blas/576054345757434; 15 Jln Mesui; small dishes RM15-18; ⏱11am-11pm Mon-Sat; 🛜; monorail Raja Chulan)

### Hakka
CHINESE $$

3  Map p26, F1

This big, long-running alfresco restaurant specialises in Hakka-style Chinese cuisine. There's lots of overpriced seasonal seafood here, but the pork and chicken dishes are reasonably priced and absolutely delicious. Try the Hakka staple of stewed pork belly on mustard greens for melt-in-the-mouth fatty goodness. The stuffed crab and tofu dishes are also excellent. (☎2143 1908; 90 Jln Raja Chulan; dishes RM18-40; ⏱11am-3pm & 6-10pm; monorail Raja Chulan)

## Top Tip

### Santouka

There are tens of thousands of Japanese living in KL (it's a popular business and retirement destination) and quality Japanese food is readily available. At Pavilion KL mall's **Tokyo Street** (Level 6) slurp tasty ramen noodles at **Santouka** (Map p26, H2; ☎2143 8878; www.santouka.co.jp; Level 6, Pavilion KL, 168 Jln Bukit Bintang; ramen set from RM26; ⏱10am-10pm; monorail Bukit Bintang), an outlet of a famous ramen stall originating from the island of Hokkaido.

### Feeka Coffee Roasters
CAFE $$

4  Map p26, C2

Set in a minimally remodelled shophouse on hip Jln Mesui, this new kid on the block has quickly become popular as both the coffee (choose from microlot beans or espresso-based drinks) and the food (from omelettes to pulled-pork sandwiches) deliver. With indoor seating lit by the traditional skywell, and a lovely tree-shaded patio area, this is a place to linger. (www.facebook.com/feeka.coffeeroasters; 19 Jln Mesui; dishes RM15-25; ⏱10am-10pm; 🛜; monorail Bukit Bintang)

### Sao Nam
VIETNAMESE $$

5  Map p26, B4

This reliable place is decorated with colourful communist propaganda posters and has a courtyard for dining

al Life

## n Alor Outdoor Eating

Restaurants on Jln Alor serve a variety of Malay, Chinese and Southeast Asian staples. Try **Wong Ah Wah** (Map p26, B5; Jln Alor; small dishes RM10-15; ⏱4pm-4am), justly famous for its seriously addictive chicken wings (RM3 per wing), or just up the street go for fiery Sichuan at **Kedai Makanan Dan Minuman TKS** (Map p26, C4; Jln Alor; small mains RM15-35; ⏱5pm-4am; monorail Bukit Bintang).

outside. The kitchen turns out huge plates of delicious Vietnamese food, garnished with basil, mint, lettuce and sweet dips. The starter *banh xeo* (a huge Vietnamese pancake with meat, seafood or vegetables) is a meal in itself. (☎2144 1225; www.saonam.com.my; 25 Tengkat Tong Shin; mains RM30-70; ⏱noon-2.30pm & 7.30-10.30pm Tue-Sun; monorail Bukit Bintang)

## Din Tai Fung                     CHINESE $$

6 🍴 Map p26, G2

One of Taiwan's most famous culinary exports is this Shanghai-style restaurant (part of a worldwide chain) that serves, with almost magical consistency, near perfect *xiao long bao* (steamed dumplings; six pieces from RM11). Also worth trying is the fried pumpkin and the drunken chicken. The restaurant is at the far back of the 6th floor of Pavilion shopping mall. (www.dintaifungmalaysia.com; Level 6, Pavilion KL, 168 Jln Bukit Bintang; mains RM11-18; ⏱10am-10pm; monorail Bukit Bintang)

## Al-Amar Lebanese Cuisine          LEBANESE $$

7 🍴 Map p26, F2

There's no shortage of restaurants in Bukit Bintang serving Middle Eastern food but few are as consistently good as Al-Amar. Choose from a tasty range of meze and grilled meats or go simple with a shawarma sandwich. There's belly dancing on Friday and Saturday nights and a Sunday lunch buffet. (☎2166 1011; www.al-amar.com; Level 6, Pavilion KL, 168 Jln Bukit Bintang; mains RM22-56; ⏱noon-midnight; monorail Bukit Bintang)

## Woods Macrobiotics          VEGETARIAN $$

8 🍴 Map p26, C5

An air of calm hangs over this operation that ticks all the organic, vegan and wholefood boxes. (Woods Bio Marche; ☎2143 1636; www.macrobiotics-malaysia.com; 28 Jln Bukit Bintang; set meals RM23; ⏱11am-9.30pm; 🍴; monorail Bukit Bintang)

## Bijan                          MALAYSIAN $$$

One of KL's best Malaysian restaurants, located next to Nerovivo (see 9 🍴 Map p26, A2), Bijan offers skilfully cooked dishes in a dining room that spills out into a tropical garden. Must-try dishes include *rendang daging* (dry beef curry with lemongrass) and *ikan panggang* (grilled skate with tamarind). (☎2031 3575; www.bijanrestaurant.com; 3 Jln Ceylon; mains RM30-90; ⏱4.30-11pm; monorail Raja Chulan)

## Nerovivo ITALIAN $$$

**9**  Map p26, A2

This long-standing Italian joint is still in top form. Enjoy a range of pastas, risottos and, of course, pizzas at this chic, partly open-air restaurant. (☏2070 3120; www.nerovivo.com; 3A Jln Ceylon; mains RM36-79; ☺noon-3pm & 6-11.30pm Sun-Fri, 6-11.30pm Sat; monorail Raja Chulan)

## Frangipani MEDITERRANEAN $$$

**10**  Map p26, B3

Mediterranean flavours predominate in this stalwart of the KL dining and party scene. The deck bar at the front opens from 6pm and serves a tapas menu. (☏2144 3001; www.frangipani.com.my; 25 Changkat Bukit Bintang; mains RM60-120; ☺7.30pm-midnight Tue-Sun; �; monorail Raja Chulan)

# Drinking

## Pisco Bar BAR

**11**  Map p26, C2

Take your pisco sour in the cosy, exposed-brick interior or the plant-filled courtyard of this slick tapas joint. The chef is half Peruvian, so naturally the ceviche here is good. (☏2142 2900; www.piscobarkl.com; 29 Jln Mesui; ☺5pm-late Tue-Sun; monorail Raja Chulan)

## Frangipani LOUNGE, CLUB

At ground level Frangipani (see **10**  Map p26, B3) has a deck bar facing the street open from 6pm, while upstairs is a chic DJ bar and lounge with regular club-night events. Friday is the official 'Frisky' gay night. Check its Facebook page for events. (☏2144 3001; www.facebook.com/FrangipaniRestaurantBar; 25 Changkat Bukit Bintang; ☺6pm-late Wed-Sat; �; monorail Raja Chulan)

## Taps Beer Bar MICROBREWERY

**12**  Map p26, C2

A very welcome addition to KL's drinking scene, Taps specialises in ale from around the world with some

✔️ Top Tip

### Healthy Options

Malaysian food is undoubtedly delicious but eating three meals a day of it can take its toll on one's waistline. When you need it, or just want it, there are some health-conscious restaurants serving organic and wholefood options. In the Golden Triangle try Woods Macrobiotics (p30) for organic box sets, and Feeka (p29) for fresh burgers and sandwiches. In KLCC head to the wholesome Living Food (p51) or the sedate RGB & the Bean Hive (p51). Fresh fruit and veggie juices (without added sugar) are also available at every mall food court. It may be a chain, but Boost is a reliable option.

## Understand

### Kuala Lumpur Cuisine

KL is a nonstop feast. You can dine in elegance or mingle with the masses at street stalls, taking your pick from a global array of cuisines.

**Chinese**
Southern Chinese flavours dominate in KL, and dishes include the taste-sensation chilli *pan mee*; try it at Kin Kin (p88). Hainanese immigrants, who were the private cooks of the British during colonial rule, developed a hybrid Western cuisine (such as chicken chops), which is still served in old-school places such as Yut Kee (p90) and the Coliseum Cafe (p90).

**Indian**
Brickfields ('Little India'), Masjid India and Chinatown are top places to sample Indian dishes. A very KL experience is snacking at a Muslim Indian-Malay eatery known as a *mamak*; try dishes such as *roti canai*, and *murtabak* (pancakes stuffed with meat) at Nasi Kandar Pelita (p50).

**Malaysian**
Head to Kampung Baru to sample the specialities of Malaysia's eastern states, such as Kelantanese *nasi kerabu* (blue rice with fried chicken); try Kak Som (p89). Malaysia's national dish, *nasi lemak* (rice boiled in coconut milk, served with fried anchovies and peanuts), is ubiquitous, but also look for *ikan bakar* (grilled fish); a good place to try it is Ikan Bakar Jalan Bellamy (p105).

**Nonya**
Common ingredients such as tamarinds, candlenuts, belacan and coconut give these Chinese-Malay fusion dishes deep flavours. Try Lima Blas (p29) or Old China Café (p72).

**Hawker**
Some of the tastiest food is found at hawker stalls. Dishes range from satay (try Zaini Satay; p93) to coconut herbal curry soup (try Keong Kee; p39).

**Markets**
Intrepid eaters shouldn't overlook *pasar* (markets). Morning markets such as Imbi Market (p24) include stalls selling dishes such as freshly griddled roti, and *chee cheong fun* (rice noodle roll; try Chee Cheong Fun Stall, p72). *Pasar malam* (night markets) are also excellent places to graze.

*Nasi kerabu* (blue rice with fried chicken)

80 different microbrews on rotation, 14 of them on tap. There's live music Thursday to Saturday at 9.30pm and an all-day happy hour on Sundays. Taps also serves pub grub (with a few Malaysian dishes) and a Sunday roast. (www.tapsbeerbar.my; One Residency, 1 Jln Nagansari; ⏰5pm-1am Mon-Sat, noon-1am Sun; 🛜; monorail Raja Chulan)

## Whisky Bar Kuala Lumpur    BAR

🚇 13    Map p26, C3

Part of the Werner's empire of restaurants and watering holes that have colonised this end of Changkat Bukit Bintang. As the name suggests, you'll find KL's largest selection of single malt, blended whiskies (including varieties from Ireland, Japan and Taiwan), and small batch American bourbons here. (www.thewhiskybarkl.com; 46 Changkat Bukit Bintang; ⏰4pm-1am Sun-Thu, 4pm-3am Fri & Sat; monorail Raja Chulan)

## Village Bar    BAR

🚇 14    Map p26, G3

The village in question is the surreal Feast Village (a collection of bars and restaurants) in the basement of the slick Starhill Gallery mall. Columns of glasses and bottles and cascades of dangling lanterns lend an *Alice in Wonderland* quality to this establishment. (Feast Floor, Starhill Gallery, 181 Jln Bukit Bintang; ⏰noon-1am; monorail Bukit Bintang)

### Blueboy Discotheque · GAY CLUB

15  Map p26, E3

Blueboy is still going strong on the KL gay scene after two decades. Friday and Saturday nights are most popular. The club is next to the Millennium Hotel. (☎2142 1067; www.facebook.com/pages/Blueboy-Discotheque-Bukit-Bintang/167616639976407; 50 Jln Sultan Ismail; ◷9pm-2am; monorail Bukit Bintang)

### Albion KL · BAR

16  Map p26, C3

Run by a British-Malay couple this restaurant and bar offers modern

### Top Tip

#### Drinking on a Budget

RM24 for a pint of cheap draught is standard across the city's bars. Happy hour specials (usually 4pm to 8pm, and sometimes all day Sunday) offer 1½ or two pints for one: Draught Guinness (the sweet syrupy local type), Kilkenny, Heineken and Tiger are your usual choices. Less-pricey canned or bottled beers can usually be found in Chinese or Indian restaurants. For two people, a decent bottle of wine is often a better deal (from both a price and quality point of view).

The **Kuala Lumpur Pub Crawl** (☎017-394 1191; www.facebook.com/KualaLumpurpubcrawl; ◷8.45pm Thu & Sat) is not necessarily a cheaper way to go drinking but it's a good way to meet fellow tipplers.

British cuisine in a gay-friendly dining and drinking venue. (☎2141 9282; www.albionkl.com; 31 Jln Berangan; ◷noon-3pm & 5-11pm Tue-Sat, noon-10.30pm Sun; monorail Bukit Bintang)

### Green Man · PUB

17  Map p26, B3

There are several British-style pubs situated along Changkat Bukit Bintang these days, but this is the original one and has a very loyal crowd. There's an all-day English breakfast on offer, steaks, and other classic pub grub dishes to be washed down with pints of draught. This is also one of the few bars open at noon (or earlier). (www.greenman.com.my; 40 Changkat Bukit Bintang; ◷11am-2am Mon-Fri, 10am-3am Sat & Sun; monorail Raja Chulan)

### Starhill Tea Salon · TEAHOUSE

18  Map p26, G3

Grand columns created from colour-coded tea caddies and luxurious sofas set an elegant tone for this tea salon, appropriately sited on Starhill Gallery's Indulge Floor. (www.starhillgallery.com; Indulge Floor, Starhill Gallery, 181 Jln Bukit Bintang; ◷10am-11pm; monorail Bukit Bintang)

### Luk Yu Tea House · TEAHOUSE

19  Map p26, G3

On the Feast Floor of Starhill Gallery but away from the heady 'Feast Village' area, the secluded Luk Yu offers fine

## Understand
### Coffee, Tea or Kopi

The story of coffee drinking in KL is tied to major historical themes: colonialism, immigration, resource extraction, language mixing and the shophouse. Hainan Chinese became expert cooks for the coffee-drinking Brits after being abandoned by their employers during the world wars, going independent (and finding cheap shophouses as the rubber industry collapsed), and calling themselves *kopitiam*, from Malay for coffee, and Chinese for shop.

Local *kopi* is roasted with butter, margarine, rice or sugar, and brewed with a muslin bag. The resulting dark, bitter drink is sweetened with condensed milk, or liquid sugar. Try it at Yut Kee (p90), Colonial Cafe (p115) or Imbi Market (p24).

KL also has a growing coffee scene that, like its predecessors, is dominated by Chinese. Try single-origin beans at Feeka (p29), VCR (p39) or RGB (p51).

Colonial rule also left KL-ites with a taste for tea. One of the best shows at a *kopitiam* is watching the tea wallah toss-pour *teh tarik* ('pulled' tea) from one pitcher to another to produce a frothy cuppa.

---

Chinese and Taiwanese teas along with dim sum and other dainty snacks. (☏2782 3850; www.starhillgallery.com; Feast Floor, Starhill Gallery, 181 Jln Bukit Bintang; ⏱noon-11pm Mon-Sat, 10am-11pm Sun; monorail Bukit Bintang)

# Entertainment

## No Black Tie
LIVE MUSIC

20 ⭐ Map p26, C2

Blink and you would miss this small live-music venue, bar and Japanese bistro, as it is hidden behind a grove of bamboo. NBT, as it's known to its faithful patrons, is owned by Malaysian concert pianist Evelyn Hii, who has a knack for finding the talented singer-songwriters, jazz bands and classical-music ensembles who play here. Live performances start from around 9.30pm. (☏2142 3737; www.noblacktie.com.my; 17 Jln Mesui; cover RM30-60; ⏱5pm-1am Mon-Sun; monorail Raja Chulan)

## GSC Pavilion KL
CINEMA

21 ⭐ Map p26, F2

Expect queues for hit movies at this multiplex in the popular Pavilion mall. This is one of the few mulitplexes in the GSC chain that has an International Screens program showing arthouse and foreign movies. (www.gsc.com.my; Level 6, Pavilion KL, 168 Jln Bukit Bintang; monorail Bukit Bintang)

# Shopping

## Royal Selangor

CRAFTS

22  🔒  Map p26, G2

This well-regarded chain of hand-crafted pewter claims origins in 1885 when a Chinese pewtersmith arrived during KL's tin-mining boom. You can still find old pieces in Central Market antique shops but the newer works on sale here are outstanding. If you have time, visit the factory and visitor centre, located 8km northeast of the city centre.
(www.royalselangor.com; Level 3, Pavilion KL, 168 Jln Bukit Bintang; ⊙10am-10pm; monorail Bukit Bintang)

---

**Local Life**

### Coffee Stain by Joseph

Enjoy excellent coffee and browse for the latest youth fashions from Japan at this third-wave **cafe** (Map p26, F3; www.facebook.com/coffeestainbyjoseph#sthash.bcGq8wQ6.dpuf; Level 3, Fahrenheit88, Jln Bukit Bintang; ⊙10am-10pm; 🛜; monorailBukit Bintang) on Level 3 of Fahrenheit88, a youth centred mall on Bukit Bintang. Single-origin beans, brewed by siphon, V60 or Chemex filters, are on offer, as well as espresso, and an interesting cold brew made from soaking cherry skins (the fruit of the coffee tree) in water.

---

## Starhill Gallery

MALL

23  🔒  Map p26, G3

With its design crossing Louis Vuitton with Louis XIV, and a basement restaurant 'village' that's a maze of dark cobbled alleys, grey slate walls and bamboo partitioning, it's worth popping into this upscale mall just for a look. Top fashion outlets such as Salvatore Ferragamo are also here, as well as an excellent culinary school, and a 'Pamper' floor for spas.
(www.starhillgallery.com; 181 Jln Bukit Bintang; ⊙10am-10pm; monorail Bukit Bintang)

## Pavilion KL

MALL

24  🔒  Map p26, G2

Pavilion sets the gold standard in KL's shopping scene. Amid the many familiar international luxury labels, there are some good local options, including unisex **British India** (www.britishindia.com.my; Great Eastern Mall, 303 Jln Ampang; ⊙10am-10pm; 🚇Ampang Park), which sells well-made linen tropical-wear for men and women. Note that when you enter the mall from the street you are already on Level 3.
(www.pavilion-kl.com; 168 Jln Bukit Bintang; ⊙10am-10pm; monorail Bukit Bintang)

## Fahrenheit88

MALL

25  🔒  Map p26, F3

Managed by Pavilion KL, this youth-orientated mall is a warren of tiny stalls and shops, many of a Japanese

## Understand

### Mall City

It's hard not to get the impression that in KL, the mall rules. Two of the world's 10 largest are here, and a quick walk down Bukit Bintang reveals a whopping eight more to choose from.

Mid-Valley Megamall is as big as a small town, while some try to look like actual towns; or in the case of Publika, a Manhattan street. Starhill Gallery, meanwhile, put a village in its basement, while Pavilion KL set up a bar street...indoors. Not to be outdone, Lot 10 (p25) reproduced a traditional chaotic food court as a clean and gleaming nostalgic fantasy (though with very good food).

The scene is as exciting and innovative to some as it is tacky and off-putting to others. No matter what, it's a distinct part of modern local life. It's also worth noting that most malls contain plenty of local products, from designer clothing to pewterware, and more surprisingly, often host museums, art galleries and non-mainstream arts festivals. Prices are high in KL, but there are frequent sales, especially around the city's many public holidays.

persuasion. Local fashion legend **Bernard Chandran** (www.bernardchandran.com) also has a boutique here on the 1st floor.

(www.fahrenheit88.com; 179 Jln Bukit Bintang; ⏱10am-10pm; monorail Bukit Bintang)

### Plaza Low Yat ELECTRONICS

 26 Map p26, D5

This is Malaysia's largest IT mall, with six floors of electronic goods and services. Head to the top-floor shops for repairs. There have been reports of credit-card details being recorded after transactions, so it's best to use cash here.

(www.plazalowyat.com/; 7 Jln Bintang off Jln Bukit Bintang; ⏱10am-10pm; monorail Bukit Bintang)

### Khoon Hooi FASHION

27 Map p26, G3

Interesting fabric textures are a signature of this up-and-coming designer's work. What sets his clothes apart is attention to detail, such as pleated belts made from zips or shifts sewn from lace.

(www.khoonhooi.com; Explore Floor, Starhill Gallery, 181 Jln Bukit Bintang; ⏱10am-10pm; monorail Bukit Bintang)

## Local Life
# Pudu

### Getting There

Pudu is south of the Golden Triangle. You can easily walk here from Bukit Bintang.

🚇**LRT** Pudu, then a three-minute walk to the market.

🚇**LRT** Hang Tuah; get off here to reverse walk.

Literally on the other side of the (monorail) tracks from the glitzy streets of Imbi, this largely Chinese neighbourhood is an excellent place to engage with KL's local urbanites. Start with the frenetic public wet market, then wander the back streets, exploring clusters of venerable shophouses, hawker centres and traditional industries.

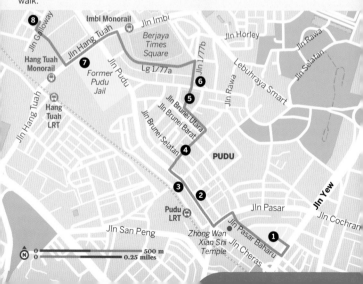

## ❶ Pudu Market

Arrive early to experience KL's largest wet (produce) **market** (Jln Pasar Baharu; ⏱4am-2pm) at its most frantic. On Jln Yew at the market's edge, check out the row of incense, joss paper and god statuary shops. Then head to humble (Pudu is not a wealthy area) **Zhong Wan Xian Shi Temple** to see where these items are used for worship.

## ❷ Glutton Street

Off the tourist radar, but renowned locally, this short alley of hawker stalls goes by the name **Glutton Street** (Pudu Wai Sek Kai; Jln Sayur; noodles RM4-7; ⏱11am-midnight, most stalls open at 5pm). Visit during the day to try the famous Hakka mee stall, right on the corner with Jln Pudu. Fried chicken and grilled fish make for great evening grazing.

## ❸ Sek Yuen Restaurant

Occupying the same beautiful, time-worn, art deco building for the past 60 years, **Sek Yuen** (☎9222 0903; 315 Jln Pudu; mains RM20-40; ⏱noon-3pm & 6-10pm Tue-Sun) is a Pudu institution. Some of the aged chefs toiling in the wood-fired kitchen have served three generations the same old-school Cantonese dishes.

## ❹ Jalan Brunei

This short street and its intersecting alleys rewards the casual wanderer. Head down Jln Brunei Selatan and Jln Brunei Barat for pre-war shophouses, inviting *kopitiam* (coffee shops), and the city's printing district. On Jln Brunei Utara check out **Restoran 168** (noodles RM3-5; ⏱10am-3pm Thu-Tue), a hole-in-the-wall famous for curry laksa and *wan tan mee*.

## ❺ Eu Yan Sang

Eu Kong opened his first Yan Sang (meaning 'caring for mankind') Chinese medicine shop in Malaysia in 1879. In addition to the company's herbal remedies, the Shaw Parade **outlet** (www.euyansang.com.my; Shaw Parade, Changkat Thambi Dollah; ⏱10am-9pm; monorail Imbi) includes a clinic for traditional *tuina* massage (body/foot RM88/56) and Chinese medicine.

## ❻ Keong Kee

This **hawker stall** (Changkat Thambi Dollah & Jln 1/77b; dishes RM4-7; ⏱4-10.30pm), set under a spreading tree in the lot across from Shaw Parade, is a Pudu institution. Try the coconut herbal curry served in a coconut shell, or the wild boar curry.

## ❼ Pudu Prison Gate

Pudu Prison was built in the late 1890s, when the area was still largely jungle (Pudu means 'half in the jungle'). It was torn down in 2012, leaving only the gate you'll pass by as a landmark.

## ❽ VCR

Set in an airy pre-war shophouse, **VCR** (www.vcr.my; 2 Jln Galloway; meals RM28-32; ⏱8.30am-10pm; 📶) serves excellent all-day breakfast, desserts, and specialty coffee. The crowd is young and diverse, but anyone will feel welcome here. Behind the shop check out Jln Sin Chew Kee, a photogenic row of colourful shophouses that look across to Bukit Bintang.

Explore

# Petronas Towers & KLCC

This is the heart of modern KL, with an impressive skyline punctuated by some of the world's tallest structures. You can gaze up at them from wooded parks, or toast the town from their sky bars and observation decks. The neighbourhood also has a few unexpected treats, from colonial bungalows and stilt houses to a jungle park with hiking trails and a great canopy walk.

# The Sights in a Day

☼ Fortify yourself with a wholefood breakfast at **Living Food** (p51) before strolling down to leafy Jln Conway to check out the heritage conservation work of **Badan Warisan Malaysia** (p48). Nearby **Kompleks Kraf** (p58) has traditional arts for sale and a good museum. Afterwards head up to KLCC Park, where towering banyan trees are the mere foreground for the **Petronas Towers** (p42).

☼ Lunch at the vegetarian **Monastery Canteen** (p51), and follow with a tour of the towers. Afterwards, head inside **Suria KLCC** (p59) for shopping, galleries and **Aquaria KLCC** (p43), or head out to Jln Ampang. Follow the stree-t west to Bukit Nanas Monorail station and the steps up to **KL Forest Eco Park** (p45), a preserved jungle right in the city.

☾ Hike up to **Menara KL** (p46) then down to Jln P Ramlee and have sundowner drinks at the **Heli Lounge Bar** (p54) followed by dinner at innovative French restaurant **Cuisine Gourmet by Nathalie** (p52). Or, at KLCC, dine at the sophisticated, elevated **Troika Sky Dining** (p53). You can drink here too, otherwise the **Sky Bar** (p54) and **Marini's on 57** (p54) both offer superb views of the towers.

## ◎ Top Sights

Petronas Towers (p42)

Menara KL (p46)

 ## Best of Kuala Lumpur

**Bars**
Troika (p53)

Heli Lounge Bar (p54)

Sky Bar (p54)

**Shopping**
Kompleks Kraf (p58)

Suria KLCC (p59)

**Street Food & Food Courts**
Dharma Realm Guan Yin Sagely Monastery Canteen (p51)

Nasi Kandar Pelita (p50)

## Getting There

🚇 **LRT** KLCC station is directly under Suria KLCC. Ampang Park station is a little east on Jln Ampang.

**Monorail** Bukit Nanas station if you want to walk up to Menara KL through the jungle (recommended).

🚌 **Bus** KL Hop-On Hop-Off buses connect all the major sights with the city's other tourist areas.

🚶 **Walking** It's pleasant to walk around the many tree-lined streets in this area.

## Top Sights
# Petronas Towers

Resembling twin silver rockets plucked from an episode of *Flash Gordon*, the Petronas Towers are the perfect symbol for the meteoric rise of the city, from tin-miners' hovels to modern shiny metropolis. They are the crowning glory of Kuala Lumpur City Center (KLCC), which covers 40 hectares of land that was once the Selangor Turf Club.

◉ Map p46, D2

www.petronastwintowers.com.my

Jln Ampang

adult/child RM80/30

🕑9am-9pm Tue-Sun, closed 1-2.30pm Fri

🚇KLCC

# Don't Miss

### Petronas Towers

Opened in 1998, the 88-storey twin towers are nearly 452m tall, and were the tallest buildings in the world from 1998 to 2004. Designed by Argentinian architect Cesar Pelli, the twin towers' floor plan is based on an eight-sided star that echoes arabesque patterns. Islamic influences are also evident in each tower's five tiers – representing the five pillars of Islam – and in the 63m masts that crown them, calling to mind the minarets of a mosque and the Star of Islam.

Tower tours are 45 minutes with a stop at the Skybridge (the world's highest bridge at 170m) on the 41st floor, with a visit to the 86th floor and the observation deck. You cannot visit the highest floors.

### KLCC Park

The park is the best vantage point for eyeballing the Petronas Towers. In the early evening it can seem like everyone in town is down here to watch the glowing towers punching up into the night sky. Every night after 8pm the Lake Symphony fountains play in front of the Suria KLCC.

### Aquaria KLCC

The highlight of this impressive **aquarium** (☎2333 1888; www.aquariaklcc.com; Concourse, KL Convention Centre; adult/child RM50/40; ⏰10.30am-8pm, last admission 7pm; ♿; ⓜKLCC) in the basement of the KL Convention Centre is its 90m underwater tunnel: view sand tiger sharks, giant gropers and more up close. Daily feeding sessions for a variety of fish and otters are complemented by ones for arapaima, electric eel and sharks on Monday, Wednesday and Saturday (see website for schedule). Free dives (RM400), cage dives (RM199), and a Sleep With Sharks (RM199) program for kids aged six to 13 are also available.

## ☑ Top Tips

▶ The easiest way to find the basement-level ticket booth and elevators to the Petronas Towers is to enter via Dewan Filharmonik Petronas (p56) and look for an escalator behind a wall to the right.

▶ Tickets go on sale at 7am and sell out fast. You can buy in advance in person for the next day, or up to a month in advance online.

▶ A 1.3km jogging track runs around KLCC Park. Arrive early morning (around 7am) to drop in to aerobics and other sports classes.

▶ Persiaran KLCC is a popular roadside spot for taking pictures of the towers. It's south of KLCC.

## ✖ Take a Break

There are scores of different dining options at Suria KLCC (p59), including two food courts. For restaurants try Little Penang Kafé (p51). The partly alfresco cafe at the Traders Hotel offers excellent sit-down views of the towers from across KLCC Park.

## Top Sights
# Menara KL

Sitting atop a dense hillock of jungle, this lofty spire is the highest telecommunications tower in Southeast Asia and one of the highest in the world. As much as the Petronas Towers it is a symbol of KL, and a top tourist attraction. Come to appreciate the phenomenal growth of the city while enjoying afternoon tea at the sky-high revolving restaurant, or explore the park's forests from trail level or along the new canopy walkway.

⊙ Map p46, A4

☐ 2020 5444

www.menarakl.com.my

2 Jln Punchak

observation deck adult/ child RM49/29, open deck adults only RM99

⊙ observation deck 9am-10pm

☐ KL Tower

# Don't Miss

## Observation Deck

Menara KL opened to the public in 1996 and although the Petronas Towers are taller structures, the telecommunications tower looks higher as its base sits already nearly 100m above sea level atop Bukit Nanas. Thus the 421m high tower actually sits 515m above sea level. A quick lift whisks visitors up to the observation decks in the bulb of the tower, the shape of which was inspired by the Malaysian spinning toy called *gasing*.

## KL Forest Eco Park

This thick lowland dipterocarp **forest** (www.forestry.gov.my; ⊙7am-6pm; ⊒KL Tower) covers 9.37 hectares in the heart of the city and is the oldest protected jungle in Malaysia (gazetted in 1906). More commonly known as Bukit Nanas (*bukit* means 'hill'), the park offers short trails up to and around Menara KL. A cool new canopy walk opened in 2014 just up from the **Forest Information Centre** (📞2026 4741; www.forestry.gov.my; Jln Raja Chulan; ⊙9am-5pm). The centre has somewhat useful maps and posters on jungle flora and fauna.

## Old Tree

During the tower's construction the base was moved slightly (at a reported cost of RM430,000) to save a 100-year-old jelutong tree. It's to the left of the tower lobby.

## Malaysia Cultural Village

Worth a visit for the reproductions of traditional *kampung* wood and attap housing from every Malaysian state. The location, along a short ridgeline running directly away from the tower lobby, also gives a unique perspective on the city: eye-level with slick high-rises hundreds of metres away, as you stand atop a mound of dense jungle.

---

## ☑ Top Tips

▶ A frequent shuttle bus (9am to 9.30pm) runs the last 500m to the tower from the gate off Jln Punchak. You can also walk this in 20 minutes.

▶ You can also get to the tower by hiking up though the forest: trails begin at the Forest Information Centre (Jln Raja Chulan), which is close to Chinatown; or off Jln Ampang at the monorail Bukit Nanas stop, a 15-minute walk from KLCC.

▶ The KL Tower Base Jump happens in September. Reserve a spot on the deck to watch and photograph the jumpers.

▶ One of the most interesting views of the tower is from the beautiful redbrick St John's Institution on Jln Bukit Nanas.

## ✖ Take a Break

Atmosphere 360 (p52) is a revolving restaurant at the top of the towers with amazing city views. Nearby, the French restaurant La Vie En Rose (p52) offers views of the tower itself from its deck.

**A** **B** **C** **D**

**For reviews see**

| | | |
|---|---|---|
| Top Sights | p42 |
| Sights | p48 |
| Eating | p50 |
| Drinking | p54 |
| Entertainment | p56 |
| Shopping | p59 |

**1**

**2**

**3**

**4**

**5**

N

0          400 m
0          0.2 miles

**KAMPUNG BARU**

Jln Sungai Baharu

Sungai Klang

**AKLEH (E12)**

Kampung Baru LRT

Jln Yap Kwan Seng

Muslim Cemetery 4

19

**Petronas Towers** 21

Jln Sultan Ismail

**Jln Ampang**

Bukit Nanas Monorail

Jln Perak

16

Jln Punchak

Jln P Ramlee

Jln Perak

Jln Pinang

Jln Perak

Sungai Klang

20

Jln Sultan Ismail

**Menara KL** 10

Jln Punchak

L & P Ramlee

14

18

Jln Perak

11

Jln P Ramlee

KL Forest Eco Park

Jln Tengah

**Raja Chulan** Monorail

13

Jln Raja Chulan

9

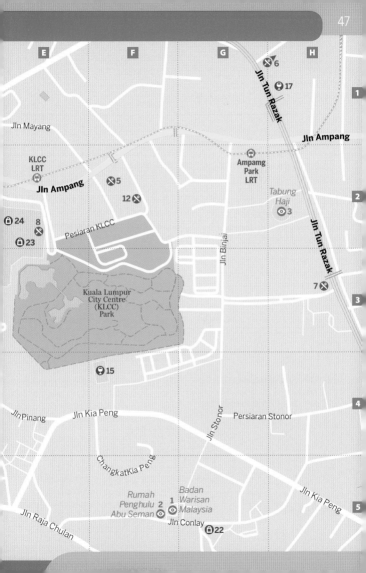

E

F

G

H

Jln Mayang

KLCC
LRT

Jln Ampang

5

12

24

8

23

Pesiaran KLCC

Jln Tun Razak

6

17

Jln Ampang

Ampang
Park
LRT

Tabung
Haji

3

Jln Tun Razak

Jln Binjai

7

Kuala Lumpur
City Centre
(KLCC)
Park

15

Jln Pinang

Jln Kia Peng

Jln Stonor

Persiaran Stonor

Changkat Kia Peng

Jln Kia Peng

Rumah
Penghulu
Abu Seman

2

Badan
Warisan
Malaysia

1

Jln Conlay

22

Jln Raja Chulan

1

2

3

4

5

# Sights

## Badan Warisan Malaysia

HISTORIC BUILDING

1 Map p46, F5

This heritage preservation society has its head office in a 1920s colonial bungalow. The building, once part of a neighbourhood of British officers' quarters, is one of the few remaining, though it's worth strolling Jln Conlay to see what's left. The trust holds exhibitions and has a small shop stocking wooden antique furniture, local handcrafted items and books.

(Heritage of Malaysia Trust; ☎2144 9273; www.badanwarisan.org.my; 2 Jln Stonor; ⏲10am-5.30pm Mon-Sat; monorail Raja Chulan)

## Top Tip

### Menara vs Petronas

Both towers offer stupendous views over this developing city, but if you want to see KL on a whim, or have forgotten to book ahead, then Menara KL is the better choice. There are rarely queues, even on weekends; finding the ticket booth is straightforward; and you can be up and down in 30 minutes and follow it up with a walk through the jungle down to Chinatown.

## Rumah Penghulu Abu Seman

HISTORIC BUILDING

2 Map p46, F5

This glorious wooden stilt-house was built in stages between 1910 and the 1930s and later moved to the grounds of Badan Warisan Malaysia. You can wander around outside tour times (and since it's built with ventilation in mind you can easily look in). Check out the stunning handcarved canoe under the house. The boat was used in religious ceremonies in Kelantan and has the head of a fantastic-looking bird carved into the prow.

(2 Jln Stonor; suggested donation RM10; ⏲tours 11am & 3pm Mon-Sat; monorail Raja Chulan)

## Muzeum Kraf

MUSEUM

Situated at the back of the Komplek Kraf shop (see 22 Map p46, G5) is this surprisingly good museum dedicated to Malaysia's traditional crafts. There are special exhibits, and regular displays of batik, wood carving, pewter, kites and drums. Exhibits are nicely accompanied by informative posters.

(Jln Conlay; adult/child RM3/1; ⏲9am-5pm; monorail Raja Chulan)

## Galeri Petronas

GALLERY

Swap consumerism for culture at this excellent art gallery showcasing contemporary photography and paintings. located in Suria KLCC (see 24 Map p46, E2), it's a bright, modern space with interesting, professionally

Rumah Penghulu Abu Seman

curated shows that change every few months.
( ☎ 2051 7770; www.galeripetronas.com.my; 3rd fl, Suria KLCC; admission free; ⏱10am-8pm Tue-Sun; 🚇KLCC)

## Petrosains
MUSEUM

Within Suria KLCC (see 24 🔒 Map p46, E2), kids and kidults can fill an educational few hours at this interactive science discovery centre with all sorts of buttons to press and levers to pull. Many of the activities and displays focus on the wonderful things that fuel has brought to Malaysia – no prizes for guessing who sponsors the museum. As a side note, 'sains' is not pronounced 'sayns' but 'science'.

(www.petrosains.com.my; Level 4, Suria KLCC; adult/child RM25/20; ⏱9.30am-5.30pm Tue-Fri, 9.30am-6.30pm Sat & Sun; 🚇KLCC)

## Tabung Haji
ARCHITECTURE

3 ◉ Map p46, H2

Designed by celebrated Malay architect Hijjas Kasturi, this distinctive tower houses the hajj funding body. The five main exterior columns represent the five pillars of Islam, while the overall structure recalls the drum used to summon pilgrims to the hajj and the shape of a traditional Arabic perfume vessel.

(201 Jln Tun Razak; 🚇Ampang Park)

## Understand
# Modern Architecture in Kuala Lumpur

Following independence there was a conscious effort to break from the ornate colonial architectural style, particularly when it came to public building. This resulted in the elegant lines of the Masjid Negara (National Mosque; p110), Stadium Merdeka (p91; built for the declaration of independence in 1957) and neighbouring Stadium Negara.

Some projects, such as the National Parliament (built in 1963 and designed by William Ivor Shipley), the National Museum, Menara Maybank and Istana Budaya (the national theatre near Lake Titiwangsa), incorporate distinctive motifs from traditional Malay architecture and art. Others, such as the beautiful Dayabumi Complex, and – later – the Petronas Towers, take their design references from Islam.

Among Malaysia's postcolonial architects of note is Hijjas Kasturi, who designed the handsome Tabung Haji (p49), the Menara Maybank buildings and the slick Bank Negara Malaysia Museum & Art Gallery (p84). Kasturi is also responsible for the somewhat ridiculous giant shark fin of Menara Telekom (clearly visible when you are in Bangsar).

## Muslim Cemetery    CEMETERY

**4** ⊙ Map p46, C2

Tucked away off Jln Ampang behind Hotel Maya, and split from Kampung Baru by a highway, is one of KL's oldest Muslim burial grounds. It's shaded by giant banyans and raintrees planted in the early 20th century. The famous film director, actor and singer P Ramlee, two of his former wives and his co-star AR Tompel are buried here. Men need to wear long pants and women a headscarf if you wish to visit.

(off Jln Ampang; ⊙7am-6pm; monorail Bukit Nanas)

# Eating

## Nasi Kandar Pelita    INDIAN, MALAYSIAN $

**5** ✕ Map p46, F2

The Jln Ampang branch of this chain of excellent *mamak* (Muslim Indian-Malay) food courts is on the ground floor of a corner bungalow on stilts. Among the 60 dishes available from the various stalls are magnificent *roti canai* (flat, flaky bread) and *hari-yali tikka* (spiced chicken with mint, cooked in the tandoor).

(www.pelita.com.my; 149 Jln Ampang; dishes RM2-8; ⊙24hr; ⊠KLCC)

## RGB & the Bean Hive
CAFE $$

6 🍴 Map p46, H1

This is what you get when a boutique coffee roaster teams with health-conscious cooks in a quiet green oasis. RGB serves excellent hand-drip coffees and espresso-based drinks as well as vegetarian sandwiches, pastas and wraps, all in a cute bungalow with an inner courtyard and big grassy yard.

(📞 2181 1329; www.facebook.com/Rather-GoodBeans; 35 Jln Damai; mains RM8-18; ⏱ 10.30am-6.30pm Mon-Fri, 10am-6pm Sat & Sun; 🛜 🖊; 🚇 Ampang Park)

## Living Food
VEGAN $$

7 🍴 Map p46, H3

Tasty and imaginative vegan and raw food is showcased at this charming cafe, oddly situated inside the Menara Tan & Tan Building (head left when you enter). But there's also plenty on the menu for the less virtuous, such as freshly made burgers and a laksa from Sarawak, where the owners hail from.

(www.livingfoodmy.com; Menara Tan & Tan, Jln Tun Razak; mains RM20-30; ⏱ 8am-7pm Mon-Fri, 9am-7pm Sat; 🛜 🖊; 🚇 Ampang Park)

## Little Penang Kafé
MALAYSIAN $$

At peak meal times expect a long line outside this Suria KLCC mall joint (see 24 🔒 Map p46, E2) serving authentic food from Penang, including special-ities such as curry mee (spicy soup noodles with prawns).

(📞 2163 0215; Level 4, Suria KLCC; mains RM12-16; ⏱ 11.30am-9.30pm; 🚇 KLCC)

## Melur & Thyme
FUSION $$

8 🍴 Map p46, E2

This appealingly designed restaurant's name, conjoining Malay and Western ingredients, hints at its game plan: offering Malay dishes alongside Western standbys such as a Caesar salad. For breakfast the coconut pancakes with caramelised honeydew melon is a very tasty precursor to a day's shopping in Suria KLCC.

(📞 2181 8001; www.melurandthyme.com; Ground fl, Suria KLCC, Jln Ampang; mains RM22-42; ⏱ 8am-10pm; 🚇 KLCC)

### ◯ Local Life
### Dharma Realm Guan Yin Sagely Monastery Canteen

Join office workers for a tasty vegetarian lunch of various fried rice and noodle dishes, dumplings and delicious *yong tau fu* (vegetables stuffed with a tofu paste) at the airy **Dharma Realm Guan Yin Sagely Monastery Canteen** (Map p48, F2; 161 Jln Ampang; meals RM6-10; ⏱ 11.30am-2pm Mon-Fri; 🚇 Ampang Park), located behind a monastery. The food contains no onions or garlic and there are drinks and fruit, too. Try to get here before noon.

## La Vie En Rose

· FRENCH $$$

9  Map p46, A5

Housed in an airy, early '50s bungalow with a terrace looking across to a row of decadently fading shophouses and the green mass of Bukit Nanas, this innovative French place is best for a lazy weekend brunch (from RM50), when there's free flow of breads and pastries from the restaurant's own bakery. (☎03-2078 3883; www.cuisine-studio.net/; 39 Jln Raja Chulan; appetisers/mains from RM24/52; ☉noon-2.30pm & 6.30-10.30pm Tue-Fri, 9.30am-2.30 & 6.30-10.30pm Sat, 9.30am-2.30pm Sun; 🛜; 🚇KL Tower)

## Atmosphere 360

MALAYSIAN, INTERNATIONAL $$$

10  Map p46, A4

Watch KL pass by from this revolving restaurant atop Menara KL (KL Tower). The lunch and dinner buffets offer ample choice of Malay dishes, though they can be hit and miss. Book ahead (you can do this online) for meals, especially sunset dining, but you can usually just drop in for high tea. Note there's a smart casual dress code. (☎2020 2020; www.atmosphere360.com.my; Menara KL, 2 Jln Puncak; buffet lunch/high tea/dinner RM76/59/170; ☉11.30am-3pm & 6.30-11pm; 🚇KL Tower)

## Cuisine Gourmet by Nathalie

FRENCH $$$

11  Map p46, B4

Having made her mark with a smaller outlet in Publika, Nathalie gets more creative with her modern French cuisine in this fine-dining space near Menara KL. If you're after a light repast, the bento-style lunches (RM45) are a bargain and the desserts sublime. (☎03-2072 4452; www.cuisinegourmetbynathalie.com; Menara Taipan, Jln Punchak; mains RM35-80; ☉noon-3pm & 6-11pm Tue-Sun; 🛜; 🚇KL Tower)

---

### Understand

### Which Floor Do You Want?

KL follows the British model for flooring, so what North Americans call the 1st floor, is ground floor here. However, almost every building has its own standards: some have Lower Ground, Ground and Upper Ground floors (and sometimes Lower and Upper Ground floors 1 and 2), Mezzanine floors, and so on. It's not uncommon to walk into a mall, ask for directions, and be told the place you want is on the 1st floor: so go up three levels. Pavilion KL is in a league of its own by labelling the floor you walk in on from the street as Level 3.

Most malls also complicate themselves with multiple sections; and then having information maps that only show shops in the section you are in. Give yourself plenty of time to find what you want when out shopping.

Atmosphere 360

## Troika Sky Dining
FRENCH, ITALIAN $$$

12   Map p46, F2

Sophisticated dining that comes with outstanding views of KLCC's glittering highrises are the highlights of the Troika complex of restaurants and bars. Try **Canteloupe** for modern French, and **Strato** for Italian that aims for homely authenticity (though we don't ever recall Mama making us Wagyu beef cheek and trotter ravioli). (☎ 2162 0886; www.troikaskydining.com; Level 23A, Tower B, The Troika, Persiaran KLCC; ; Ampang Park)

# Drinking

## Fuego
BAR

Part of Troika (see 12   Map p46, F2), Fuego shares the same sophisticated ambience and jaw-dropping views across the KLCC park as the fine-dining restaurants. The bar specialises in innovative cocktails and tapas, while its sister venue, **Claret**, open from 4pm to 1am, offers a curated wine list. (☎ 2162 0886; www.troikaskydining.com; Level 23A, Tower B, The Troika, Persiaran KLCC; ⏰ 6pm-midnight; Ampang Park)

### ...nge Bar

COCKTAIL BAR

**13**  Map p46, D5

Nothing besides your lychee martini and the cocktail waiter stands between you and the edge of the helipad at KL's most thrilling rooftop bar. Yep, 34 floors up and this outdoor joint has no railing. Only come if the weather's fine, as the views are 360-degrees amazing, but do be careful. (2110 5034; www.facebook.com/Helil-oungebar; Level 34, Menara KH, Jln Sultan Ishmail; ⏱6pm-midnight Mon-Wed, to 2am Thu, to 3am Fri & Sat; 🛜; monorail Raja Chulan)

### Apartment Downtown

CAFE, BAR

As one of the least generic looking of the semi-outdoor restaurants and bars facing the fountains of KLCC (see **24** 🔒  Map p46, E2), the Apartment pulls in a younger and less touristy crowd. A recent renovation created more space between tables. (www.atheapartment.com; Jln Ampang, 1st fl, Suria KLCC; ⏱10am-midnight; 🚇KLCC)

### Luna Bar

BAR

**14**  Map p46, B4

A twinkling view of KL's skyline is guaranteed at this sophisticated rooftop bar surrounding a swimming pool. (2332 7777; www.facebook.com/lunabarkl; 34th fl, Pacific Regency Hotel Suites, Jln Punchak, off Jln P Ramlee; ⏱10am-1am Sun-Thu, to 3am Fri & Sat; 🛜; 🚇KL Tower)

### Sky Bar

BAR

**15**  Map p46, F4

Head to the rooftop pool area of this hotel for a grand circle view across to the Petronas Towers – it's the perfect spot for sundowner cocktails or late-night flutes of bubbly. (2332 9888; www.skybar.com.my; Level 33, Traders Hotel; ⏱10am-1am Sun-Thu, to 3am Fri & Sat; 🚇KLCC)

### Marini's on 57

BAR

**16** Map p46, D3

This is about as close as you can get to eyeballing the upper levels of the Petronas Towers from a bar. The stellar views are complemented by a sleek interior design and attentive service. When booking (advised) be aware that it's the lively bar not the laid-back

---

☑️ Top Tip

**Jalan Ampang**

On the northern border of KLCC Park is Jln Ampang, a historic street that once led from the mansions of the tin tycoons to the mines themselves out in Ampang (Ampang means 'dam', a reference to the dams created during the mining process). Today the wide street is still lined with rain-trees and banyans planted over a hundred years ago, though only a handful of the old bungalows remain, including the ones used for the Malaysian Tourism Centre and the gorgeous Pakistan High Commission across the road.

## Understand
# Gay & Lesbian Kuala Lumpur

Malaysia is a predominantly Muslim country and the level of tolerance for homosexuality is vastly different from its neighbours. Sex between men is illegal at any age and sharia Islamic laws also forbid cross-dressing. Fortunately, outright persecution of gays and lesbians is rare; the sodomy case against opposition leader Ibrahim Anwar that made headlnes in 2014 was politically motivated. Nonetheless, gay and lesbian travellers should avoid behaviour that may attract unwanted attention – Malaysians are quite conservative about any displays of public affection.

That said, there is, a bit surprisingly, a fairly open gay scene in KL, with several established gay dance nights: the main ones are at Frangipani (p31) and Blueboy (p34). Reggae Bar (p74) in Chinatown is also gay-friendly, as is the modern British restaurant and pub Albion KL (p34). Start looking for information on www.utopia-asia.com or www.fridae.com, both of which provide good coverage of LGBT events and activities across Asia.

whisky lounge that has the view of the towers.

(📞2386 6030; www.marinis57.com; Level 57, Menara 3, Petronas KLCC; ⏰5pm-1.30am Sun-Thu, to 3am Fri & Sat; 🚇KLCC)

## Tate                                    COCKTAIL BAR

**17** 🚇 Map p46, H1

It's bordering on self-mockery to have a 'secret' speakeasy cocktail bar in a shopping mall, but once you get past that, Tate's sophisticated atmosphere, complete with cushy leather armchairs and a great cocktail menu, is perfect for a relaxing late night drink.

(www.thebiggroup.co; ground fl, Intermark, 182 Jln Tun Razak; ⏰5pm-2am Mon-Sat; 🛜; 🚇Ampang Park)

## Neo Tamarind                          BAR

**18** 🚇 Map p46, C4

Next to its sister operation, Burmese-Thai restaurant Tamarind Hill, this sophisticated restaurant–bar feels like a slice of Bali in the heart of KL. Sip cocktails by flickering lights and a waterfall running the length of the long bar. The Thai and Indochinese food is also lovely should you want to start with dinner.

(www.samadhiretreats.com; 19 Jln Sultan Ismail; ⏰5pm-midnight; monorail Raja Chulan)

## Zouk                                   CLUB

**19** 🚇 Map p46, C2

This popular club has spaces to suit everyone and a line-up of top local and international DJs. In addition to the two-level main venue, there's the more

PAUL GADD/CORBIS ©

Dewan Filharmonik Petronas

sophisticated Velvet Underground for the older, well-heeled clubber; Phuture for hip-hop; and the rooftop bar Aristo, which is open from 6pm. Cover charges vary between venues.
(www.zoukclub.com.my; 113 Jln Ampang; ⊙9pm-3am Tue-Sun; monorail Bukit Nanas)

# Entertainment

## KL Live                    LIVE MUSIC

20 ⭐  Map p46, C4

One of the best things to happen to KL's live-music scene has been the opening of this spacious venue, which has been packing in rock and pop fans

with an impressive line-up of overseas and local big-name artists and DJs.
(www.kl-live.com.my; 1st fl, Life Centre, 20 Jln Sultan Ismail; monorail Raja Chulan)

## Dewan Filharmonik Petronas          CONCERT VENUE

21 ⭐  Map p46, D2

Don't miss the chance to attend a show at this concert hall which is at the base of the Petronas Towers. The polished Malaysian Philharmonic Orchestra plays here (usually on Friday and Saturday evenings and Sunday matinees), as do other local and international ensembles. There is a dress code that needs to be observed.
(📞2051 7007; mpo.com.my/; Box Office, Tower 2, Petronas Towers, KLCC; ⊙box office 10am-6pm Mon-Sat; 🚇KLCC)

## Time Out Comedy Thursday          COMEDY

It's always a packed house for this monthly stand-up gig at Zouk (see 19 🎙 Map p46, C2), which has been running continuously since 2008.
(📞2166 6650; www.timeoutkl.com; Zouk Club, 113 Jln Ampang; cover RM25; ⊙8.30pm 1st Thu of month; monorail Bukit Nanas)

## TGV Cineplex          CINEMA

Take your pick from the offerings at this 12-screen multiplex located in Suria KLCC (see 24 🔒 Map p46, E2). Book in advance or be prepared to queue, particularly at weekends.
(www.tgv.com.my/cinemas/suria-klcc; Level 3, Suria KLCC; 🚇KLCC)

## Understand

# The Cultural Makeup of Kuala Lumpur

Kuala Lumpur is a multicultural potpourri. Wander around Chinatown on a Sunday or Bukit Bintang on any night of the week and it's almost as if you've touched down in a convention of the United Nations. The main ethnic groups may be Malays, Chinese and Indians, but there are also communities of Indonesians and Thais (many of whom live in Kampung Baru) as well as Pakistanis, Bangladeshis, Nepalis and Burmese. Scores of Middle Eastern folk have also settled here, and Japanese are numerous enough to warrant their own school in Mont Kiara, and a vibrant restaurant scene. Smaller communities include the Korean enclave in Ampang and the pockets of Western professionals and retirees around Bangsar and KLCC. In all, these smaller foreign communities comprise anywhere from 2% to 9% of the city's population.

### Malays

Like almost everyone else in KL, most of the city's Malay residents hail from beyond the city's borders. Many still hanker after the spirit of the communal *kampung* (village) and, come any long weekend, the roads out of KL are jammed with carloads of city families headed to their home village. Today about 40% of the population of KL is Malay.

### Chinese

The very birth of KL in the 19th century coincided with an influx of Chinese immigrants, mainly Hakka and Cantonese who came to work the tin mines. Among the ethnic groups that followed were the Hainanese, who became renowned cooks for the British – KL's Hainan fare is legendary. Today Chinese make up about 40% of the population of the city and are prominent in business, though religious customs still govern much of home life.

### Indians

Like the Chinese, Indians in KL (who comprise about 10% of the population) trace their ancestry to many parts of the motherland (and also Sri Lanka) and practise different cultural traditions, especially with respect to religion: there are Hindus, Muslims, Sikhs, Christians and more. Most KL Indians are Tamils, with roots in Tamil Nadu in southern India, where Hindu traditions are strong.

Understand

## Talking the Talk

As the capital of a former British colony, Kuala Lumpur is generally an easy place to travel for English-speakers, but you'll have to get used to the local patois, which includes plenty of Mandarin, Cantonese, Hokkien, Tamil and Bahasa words and phrases. Abbreviations are also a way of life here, such as KL (for Kuala Lumpur) or PJ (Petaling Jaya).

Keep an ear out for sentence-ending words borrowed from Chinese grammar. Most do not add meaning (as in Chinese) but a tone or mood to what was said. Common expressions include:

**Lah** Common suffix used to affirm a statement. 'Don't be stupid, *lah*.'

**Leh** Hard to distinguish from *lah* but softens what was said. 'Give me, *leh*.'

**Can** Used to mean yes and often repeated with *lah* added, eg 'Can you come pick me up?' 'Can can, *lah*.'

**Got** Used for all tenses of the verb 'to have', eg 'Got noodles in the soup?' 'Got money.'

**Meh** An expression of scepticism, eg 'Really meh?'

**Malaysia boleh** 'Malaysia can do it,' but often used now to refer to under-the-table activities, eg 'Can I get cheap duty-free liquor in town?' 'Can. Malaysia *boleh*.'

# Shopping

## Kompleks Kraf Kuala Lumpur

ARTS, CRAFTS

**22**  Map p46, G5

A government enterprise, this huge complex mainly caters to people on coach tours, but it's worth a visit to browse the shops and stalls selling wood carvings, pewter, basketware, glassware and ceramics and especially to visit the attached Muzeum Kraf (p48). It's a pleasant walk here from KLCC Park.

( ☎ 2162 7533; www.kraftangan.gov.my/101/ main/content/68; Jln Conlay; ⏰ 9am-8pm Mon-Fri, to 7pm Sat & Sun; monorail Raja Chulan, then taxi)

## Ang Eng

CLOTHING

**23** Map p46, E2

Ang Eng has been making Nonya *kebaya* (a traditional colourful blouse in the Peranakan style) since 1955, and

is still highly recommended by the Chinese community.
(☎2161 2324; Level 2, Suria KLCC, Jln Ampang; ☺10am-10pm; 🚇KLCC)

## Suria KLCC
MALL

24 🔒 Map p46, E2

Even if shopping bores you to tears, you're sure to find something to interest you at this fine shopping complex at the foot of the Petronas Towers, strong on both local and international brands.
(www.suriaklcc.com.my; KLCC, Jln Ampang; ☺10am-10pm; 🚇KLCC)

### Aseana
FASHION

Billed as Malaysia's 'largest luxury multi-brand boutique' and located at Suria KLCC (see 24 🔒 Map p46, E2),

Aseana is noted for accessories, bags, jewellery, and an extensive selection from international and local fashion luminaries such as Malaysian **Farah Khan** (www.farahkhan.com), who specialises in beaded and sequined glamour-wear.
(www.melium.com; Ground fl, Suria KLCC, Jln Ampang; ☺10am-10pm; 🚇KLCC)

### Tenmoku Pottery
HOMEWARES

With its kilns based near Batu Caves and this shop located at Suria KLCC (see 24 🔒 Map p46, E2), Tenmoku Pottery specialises in vases, bowls and other ceramics inspired by natural forms.
(www.tenmokupottery.com.my; Level 3, Suria KLCC, Jln Ampang; ☺10am-10pm; 🚇KLCC)

Explore

# Chinatown & Merdeka Square

KL's Chinatown is as classic as they come, with rows of ageing shop-houses and art deco mansions punctuated with temples, gold merchants and back-alley fried-noodle vendors. But with its mosques and Hindu temples it's more multicultural than most. Adjacent Merdeka (Independence) Square was once the centre of British colonial power, and has the inspiring Indo-Saracenic architecture to show for it.

# The Sights in a Day

☀ Begin your day with a fusion breakfast at **LOKL** (p73) then stroll through the **Old High Court Building** (p68) verandah, which ends with your first view of **Merdeka Square** (p62). On Monday, Wednesday and Saturday, join the **heritage walk** (p67), otherwise stop in at **KL City Gallery** (p63) for a rundown on the city's history, then explore the surrounding Indo-Saracenic buildings and museums on your own. Get to **Masjid Jamek** (p66) before it closes at 12.30pm.

☀ Next head over to Chinatown, stopping at **Medan Pasar** (p69), where KL began. For lunch, try the canteen **Restoran Yusoof dan Zakhir** (p71), or **Peter Hoe Beyond** (p73) in the Lee Rubber Building. Plan to spend a few hours in **Central Market** (p67), shopping, browsing, and exploring the **Museum of Ethnic Arts** (p68). Afterwards, visit the area's key temples, both Indian and Chinese. Wind down with an ice coffee at **Moontree House** (p74).

☾ Dine around the corner at **Old China Café** (p72), or go old-school at **Kim Lian Kee** (p71) on Petaling St. Wander the frenetic **night market** (p79), then enjoy an outdoor beer and BBQ on Jln Sultan. For fancier digs head to the speakeasy **Omakase + Appreciate** (p74).

## ◉ Top Sights
Merdeka Square (p62)

## ♥ Best of Kuala Lumpur

**Street Food & Food Courts**
Madras Lane Hawkers (p72)

Hong Ngek (p69)

Restoran Yusoof dan Zakhir (p71)

**Shopping**
Peter Hoe Beyond (p78)

Central Market (p78)

Museum of Ethnic Arts (p68)

**Entertainment**
Kelantan Shadow Puppet Play (p76)

Panggung Bandaraya (p76)

Petaling Street Art House (p77)

**For Free**
KL City Gallery (p63)

Masjid Jamek (p66)

Museum Of Ethnic Arts (p68)

## Getting There

🚇 **LRT** Pasar Seni and Masjid Jamek are the most convenient stations for Chinatown and Mederka Square.

🚌 **Bus** KL Hop-On Hop-Off buses connect Merdeka Square with Central Market.

🚶 **Walking** Chinatown is compact and you can easily walk the entire area. It's often faster than a taxi or bus because of the narrow traffic-snarled streets.

## Top Sights
# Merdeka Square

Once the green nucleus of colonial power on the Malay Peninsula, Merdeka (which means independence) became fixed in the national consciousness at midnight on 31 August 1957 when the British flag was lowered and the Malayan States flag hoisted up a towering flagpole. The square is ringed by heritage buildings, and people come here to learn about the city's history as much as to admire the grand colonial architecture. With few high-rises visible from the square, time does seem to stand still here.

⊙ Map p64, A2

Dataran Merdeka

🚇 Masjid Jamek

Sultan Abdul Samad Building

# Don't Miss

### Royal Selangor Club

The square is surrounded by some of KL's best colonial-era buildings, including the Tudor-style **Royal Selangor Club** (www.rscweb.my; Jln Raja; Masjid Jamek). Built in 1884, this exclusive social club for the KL elite is where social running club Hash House Harriers was formed in 1938.

### Sultan Abdul Samad Building

On one side of the square is a row of iconic buildings, including the **Sultan Abdul Samad Building** (Jln Raja; Masjid Jamek). Built in 1897, it was the first public building in Malaysia designed in the Mughal (or Indo-Saracenic) style, and it influenced a rash of others across the city. The building to the right is the old General Post Office.

### National Textiles Museum

This excellent **museum** (Muzium Tekstil Negara; 2694 3457; www.muziumtekstilnegara.gov.my; Jln Sultan Hishamuddin; admission free; 9am-6pm; Masjid Jamek) occupies another elegant Mughal-style building. The lower floors cover the history of textiles, in particular Malaysian fabrics such as *songket* (silk with gold threading), and the traditional process used in manufacturing. The upper floors cover Malaysian fabrics and design motifs in greater detail, as well as jewellery and headgear.

### KL City Gallery

Get a quick but detailed overview of the city's history, and pick up a folder full of travel information, at this official **tourism information centre** (2691 1382; www.klcitygallery.com; 27 Jln Raja, Dataran Merdeka; admission RM5; 9am-6.30pm; Masjid Jamek) set in the former Government Printing Office (built 1898). On the 2nd floor is a large scale model of Kuala Lumpur.

## ☑ To...

▶ Aim fo...
or late-afternoon visit. The midday sun always feels particularly fierce here.

▶ With the KL City Gallery (the official city tourism information centre) here, the square is the best place to get orientated and informed on your first day in town; pick up a walking tour map to explore all the surrounding colonial buildings.

▶ The lovely Lake Gardens are just a short walk or bike ride up Jln Raja Laut.

## ✗ Take a Break

There's a cafe in KL City Gallery, but there's more to choose from in Chinatown, just a few minutes walk away. Try the block on Jln Tun HS Lee between Jln Tun Perak and Jln Gereja. Hong Ngek (p69) offers traditional *kopitiam* comfort food, while LOKL (p73) offers much the same in more hipper environs.

For reviews see

| | | |
|---|---|---|
| ◎ | Top Sights | p62 |
| ◉ | Sights | p66 |
| ✕ | Eating | p69 |
| ◒ | Drinking | p74 |
| ⊕ | Entertainment | p76 |
| ⊙ | Shopping | p78 |

Jln Cangkat Stadium

Jln Stadium

Stadium
Merdeka ◎ 11

Jln Hang Jebat

Jln Hang Jebat

Maharajalela
Ⓜ Monorail

Jln Maharajalela

Jln Sultan

1 Chan She Shu Yuen Clan
◎ Association Temple

Jln Belfield

Petaling Street Market

Jln Stadium

Jln Akar

Bulatan Merdeka

Jln Attap

Jln Kampong

Jln Sultan

38 ◉
Petaling Street Market

✕ 16 19

18 ✕

25 ◉
Jln Hang Lekir    9 Guandi
◎ Temple
34 ◉ 21 ✕    Madras La
CHINATOWN

Madras La

37 ◉

27 ◉ 26 ◉

20 ✕

Jln Panggong

Jln Sultan

2 ◎
Sri
Mahamariamman
Temple

Jln HS Lee

Jln Hang Kasturi

Jln Kinabalu

Jln Benteng

Pasar
Seni
LRT Ⓜ

Sungai Klang

Jln Sultan Hishamuddin

Jln Tun Sambanthan

Kuala
Lumpur Ⓚ

Jln Sultan Hishamuddin

Jln Tugu

N Ⓜ

200 m
0.1 miles

5
6
7
8

A
B
C
D
E

# Sights

### Chan She Shu Yuen Clan Association Temple
TEMPLE

1  Map p64, D7

Opened in 1906 to serve immigrants with the surname Chan, this Cantonese-style temple is a beauty. Decorative panels of 100-year-old Shek Wan pottery adorn the facade and eaves, while side gables swirl like giant waves. Inside the high-ceilinged main hall, an altar enshrines the three ancestors of the Chan clan. Note a current restoration project is replacing the green-coloured roof tiles with grey ones in deference to the original model ancestral temple in Guangzhou, China.

( ✆2078 1461; Jln Petaling; admission free; ◷9am-6pm; monorail Maharajalela)

### Sri Mahamariamman Temple
HINDU TEMPLE

2  Map p64, C6

This lively Hindu temple – the oldest in Malaysia and rumoured to be the

## Top Tip

### Masjid Jamek at Night
Masjid Jamek is stunning when lit up at night, and one of the best places to view it is from the LRT Masjid Jamek station. Best viewing spots are at the glass wall on the way up to the platforms, and on the platforms themselves.

richest – was founded in 1873. Mariamman is the South Indian mother goddess, also known as Parvati. Her shrine is at the back of the complex. On the left sits a shrine to the elephant-headed Ganesh, and on the right one to Lord Murugan. During the Thaipusam festival, Lord Murugan is transported to Batu Caves from the temple on a silver chariot.

(163 Jln Tun HS Lee; admission free; ◷6am-8.30pm, till 9.30pm Fri; 🚇Pasar Seni)

### Sin Sze Si Ya Temple
TEMPLE

3  Map p64, C4

Kuala Lumpur's oldest Chinese temple was built on the instructions of Kapitan Yap Ah Loy and is dedicated to Sin Sze Ya and Si Sze Ya, two Chinese immigrants instrumental in Yap's ascension to Kapitan status. Several beautiful objects decorate the temple, including two hanging carved panels, but the best feature is the almost frontier-like atmosphere. This is still an important temple for the community, much as it was in 1864 when 10,000 people turned out for opening day.

(Jln Tun HS Lee; admission free; ◷7am-5pm; 🚇Pasar Seni)

### Masjid Jamek
MOSQUE

4  Map p64, B2

This onion-domed mosque packs a double aesthetic punch. Gracefully designed in Mughal style, it's situated at the confluence of two rivers, the Gombak and Klang. Built in

Sri Mahamariamman Temple

1907 based on the design of British architect AB Hubback, it was the first brick mosque in Malaysia and the city's centre of Islamic worship until the opening of the National Mosque in 1965. You can visit inside outside prayer times, but dress conservatively and remember to remove your shoes before entering.

(Friday Mosque; off Jln Tun Perak; admission free; ⏰9am-12.30pm & 2.30-4pm, closed Fri; 🚇Masjid Jamek)

### Dataran Merdeka Heritage Walk

WALKING TOUR

5 ◉ Map p64, A2

This free walk, taking in 11 heritage sights around Merdeka Square, runs from 9am to 11.45am every Monday, Wednesday and Saturday, starting at the KL City Gallery in the square. (📞2698 0332; Merdeka Sq; admission free)

### Central Market

MARKET

6 ◉ Map p64, B4

One of KL's most popular sights, this 1930s art deco building (a former wet market) was rescued from demolition in the 1980s and transformed into an arts and crafts centre aimed at tourists. Nonetheless, there are some excellent shops, good restaurants, and a brilliant museum in the annexe. The adjacent Kasturi Walk – the arch is a series of *wau bulan* (kites) is bordered by a row of handsome restored

shophouses. Thirty-minute dance performances are held nightly at 9pm except Fridays.
(www.centralmarket.com.my; Jln Hang Kasturi; ◷10am-10pm; 🚇Pasar Seni)

## Museum of Ethnic Arts        MUSEUM

7 ◉ Map p64, B4

This extraordinary private collection of tribal arts from Borneo is mixed with Nonya ceramics, Tibetan thangka paintings, Chinese paintings and porcelain, embroidered wall hangings, hand-carved boxes and doors, and all manner of delights from Malaysia and the region. Almost everything is for sale here.
(📞2301 1468; 2nd fl, The Annexe, 10 Jln Hang Kasturi; admission free; ◷10.30am-7pm; 🚇Masjid Jamek)

### Local Life
#### Chetty Street
From the Masjid Jamek LRT station walk one block southeast to **Lebuh Ampang**, formerly known as Chetty St, after the Chettiars of South India. Chettiars were a merchant caste, and in KL's early days, before proper banks, they acted as moneylenders. That traditional business is more faded than the paint on many of the street's old shophouses, but it's still worth a visit to this historic part of the old city. A few moneychangers remain, as do gold-sellers, Indian cafes, and street vendors selling sweets and flower garlands.

## Old High Court Building        HISTORIC BUILDING

8 ◉ Map p64, B1

You're likely to walk down the arched verandah of this handsome, AB Hubbard–designed heritage building opened in 1915, on the way to Merdeka Square from the Masjid Jamek LRT station. Cross the street to admire the rows of ogee arches of the ground floor, the keyhole arches on the 1st floor, and the rooftop cupolas.
(Jln Benteng; 🚇Masjid Jamek)

## Guandi Temple        TEMPLE

9 ◉ Map p64, C5

Founded in 1886, this atmospheric temple is dedicated to Guandi, a historical Chinese general known as the Taoist god of war, but more commonly worshipped as the patron of righteous brotherhoods: he is in fact patron of both police forces and triad gangs. The temple's high ceilings, red walls, tiled eaves and pointy gable ends give it a distinctive look that's great for photos, though there are few details to admire up close.
(Jln Tun HS Lee; ◷7am-5pm; 🚇Pasar Seni)

## St Mary's Anglican Cathedral        CHURCH

10 ◉ Map p64, A1

This handsome Gothic-revival English country church was designed by government architect AC Norman and erected in 1894. It was the first brick church in Malaysia and it still maintains a small Anglican congregation. Inside is a fine pipe-organ built in 1895 by Henry Willis (though since heavily restored), the Englishman responsible for the organ in St Paul's Cathedral in London. It's now dedicated to Sir Henry Gurney, the British high commissioner to Malaya, assassinated in 1951 during the Emergency.

(📞2692 8672; www.stmaryscathedral.org.my; Jln Raja; 🚇Masjid Jamek)

### Stadium Merdeka   HISTORIC BUILDING

11  Map p64, E8

Built for the declaration of independence in 1957, this open-air stadium is where Malaysia's first prime minister, Tunku Abdul Rahman, famously punched his fist in the air seven times shouting 'Merdeka!' (Independence!). Other big events during its history include a boxing match between Muhammad Ali and Joe Bugner, and a concert by Michael Jackson. There are panoramic views of the city from the grandstands and a couple of evocative photographic murals in the entrance hall.

(Jln Stadium; monorail Maharajalela)

### St John's Cathedral   CHURCH

12  Map p64, D2

This twin-spired structure (established 1883) is the only Catholic cathedral in KL. Further up the road is the striking red-brick **St John's Institute**, which seems a mix of colonial Spanish and Japanese-Rennaisance architec-

### Top Tip
#### KL by Cycle
Cycling is a great way to get around Merdeka Square, Chinatown and the Lake Gardens. Rent basic **bikes** (Map p69, A3) at the information desk in the underground mall across from the KL City Gallery. Rentals include a helmet.

ture. From here you can also see both the Petronas Towers and Menara KL peeking over Bukit Nanas.

(Jln Bukit Bintang; 🚇Masjid Jamek)

### Medan Pasar   SQUARE

13  Map p64, B3

Recently transformed into a pedestrian square, Medan Pasar (which translates as Market Square) was once the heart of Chinatown. Kapitan Yap Ah Loy lived here, and in addition to holding the city's wet market, it was a place of brothels and illegal gambling dens (now long gone). In the centre stands an art deco clock tower built in 1937 to commemorate the coronation of King George IV.

(🚇Masjid Jamek)

## Eating

### Hong Ngek   CHINESE $

14  Map p64, C3

This long-running Hokkien restaurant serves expertly made fried *bee hoon*

## Understand
## Colonial Architecture

Chinatown and Merdeka Square are centre stage for some of KL's best colonial architecture.

### Indo-Saracenic (Mughal)

Grand civic buildings around Merdeka Square signalled the British desire to stamp their colonial mark on the city. It isn't exactly clear why, but government architects such as AB Hubback and AC Norman designed masterpieces that blended European elements with the Mughal style they had observed in India. Some obvious features of this style are corner towers and slim minarets, domes, chatris (plates under the domes), repetitive use of arches (keyhole, horseshoe and ogee), and (usually) brick facades.

The style did not remain in fashion for long. The Sultan Abdul Samad Building, the first of its kind, was built in 1897, while the last, the KTM Headquarters (across from the grand Old KL Train Station), was finished in 1917.

### Shophouses, Bungalows & Mansions

Quintessential icons of colonial Straits Chinese architecture across Southeast Asia, shophouses began to appear from the 1880s as the city rebuilt itself after a great fire destroyed all the wood and attap housing.

The typical shophouse has a shop at the front with living quarters above and to the rear. Constructed in terraces, each unit is long and narrow, approximately 6m by 30m, sometimes as long as 60m. Inner courtyards provide ventilation, while arcade walkways (the so-called 'five-foot way') at the front provide protection from rain and harsh sunlight. The uniform arcade was first imposed in Singapore by order of Sir Stamford Raffles.

As KL became more prosperous, two-storey shophouses began to add an extra floor and redo their facades in a range of styles, from neoclassical to Dutch Patrician to art deco. Some of the best remaining rows are on Jln Hang Kasturi, Medan Pasar and Jln Sin Chew Kee behind VCR.

In the early 20th century Chinese tin and rubber merchants lined streets such as Jln Ampang with detached two-storey bungalows that could be accessed by horse-drawn carriage. The wealthiest constructed grand mansions such as Loke Mansion (p86) and the former Royal Museum (p119) that combined European classical architectural forms with Chinese decorative motifs.

PETER HORREE/ALAMY ©

Restaurants along Petaling Street

(vermicelli noodles), ginger duck rice, crab balls and succulent pork ribs stewed in Guinness. There's air-con upstairs, but it's more interesting to watch the world go by at a table on the naturally ventilated street level. The joint sometimes closes at 5.30pm, so don't be late for dinner. (50 Jln Tun HS Lee; dishes RM6-7.50; ⏱10am-7pm Mon-Sat; 🚇Masjid Jamek)

### Restoran Yusoof dan Zakhir
INDIAN $

**15** 🍴 Map p64, B4

This huge banana-yellow and palm-tree-green canteen opposite Central Market on the pedestrian street serves delicious *mamak* (Muslim Indian-

Malay) food; perfect for a roti or dosa and a curry sauce snack. The fresh fruit drinks are also good here. (Jln Hang Kasturi; dishes RM2-8; ⏱6am-midnight; 🚇Pasar Seni)

### Kim Lian Kee
NOODLES $

**16** 🍴 Map p64, C5

Reputedly serving the best Hokkien mee in the city for the past 80 years, this old-school restaurant sits right in the heart of Petaling Street Market. Take your noodles upstairs for a view over the street or downstairs alleyside. (49 Jln Petaling; Hokkien mee RM8, other dishes RM15-35; ⏱5pm-4am; 🚇Kota Raya)

Local Life

## Outdoor Eating in Chinatown

Along Jln Sultan, restaurants offer roadside BBQ, seafood, and cheap(ish) beers at night. Morning and early afternoon head to Madras Lane (enter beside Guandi Temple) for curry laksa, *bak kut teh* (pork rib soup), *yong tau fu* (vegetables stuffed with tofu) as well as other local specialities.

Some reputable hawker stalls are crammed in tiny alleyways. **Lian Bee** (Map p64, C4; Jln Tun Tan Chen Lock; ⊙4.30-10pm Wed-Mon), beside the famous Kedai Kopi Lai Foong hawker stall court on Jln Tun Tan Chen Lock, has been selling well-loved Hokkien mee since the 1950s.

## Restoran Santa INDIAN $

17  Map p64, D2

You won't find any Christmas delights at this no-frills cafe but freshly made chapatis well loved by the surrounding Indian community. Paired with a side dish of curried chickpeas or dhal they are the perfect fast cheap snack if you need a break any time of day.

(11 Jln Tun HS Lee; chapatis RM1.50; ⊙6.30am-6.30pm Mon-Fri, 6.30am-3pm Sat; 🚇Masjid Jamek)

## Madras Lane Hawkers HAWKER $

18  Map p64, C5

Enter beside the Guandi Temple to find this alley of hawker stalls. It's best visited for breakfast or lunch, with standout operators including the one offering 10 types of *yong tau fu* (vegetables stuffed with tofu and a fish and pork paste). The *bah kuh teh* (pork rib soup) and curry laksa stalls are also good.

(Madras Lane; noodles RM5; ⊙8am-4pm Tue-Sun; 🚇Pasar Seni)

## Chee Cheong Fun Stall CHINESE $

19  Map p64, C5

Just off Petaling St on Jln Hang Lekir, in the heart of the pedestrian area, this stall has been soothing early morning appetites for decades with melt-in-the-mouth *chee cheong fun* (rice noodles) doused with sweet and spicy sauces and a sprinkle of sesame seeds. A few metres down is the Cantonese congee (rice porridge) stall Hon Kee.

(Cnr Jln Petaling & Jln Hang Lekir; noodles RM4-6; ⊙7am-4pm Thu-Tue; 🖉; 🚇Kota Raya)

## Old China Café MALAYSIAN, NONYA $$

20  Map p64, C7

Housed in an old guild hall of a laundry association, this restaurant captures some of the charm of old KL with its high walls covered with bric-a-brac, and round marbletop tables. Try the beef rendang, the succulent Nonya fried chicken, and some unusual but tasty appetisers such as the stuffed top hats (a small pastry shaped like a hat in which you stuff veggies). (📞2072 5915; www.oldchina.com.my; 11 Jln Balai Polis; dishes RM11-32; ⏱11am-11pm; 🚇Pasar Seni)

## Peter Hoe Beyond Cafe
INTERNATIONAL $$

21  Map p64, C5

You may find the affable Mr Hoe himself serving at this supremely relaxing cafe in the corner of an arts-and-crafts shop in the historic Lee Rubber Building. Tuck into a great lunch of delicious quiche with masses of fresh salad, or just enjoy a cake and coffee in between forays around the stylishly merchandised retail space. (2nd fl, Lee Rubber Bldg, 145 Jln Tun HS Lee; mains RM20-39; ⏱10am-7pm, meals noon-3; 📶; 🚇Pasar Seni)

## LOKL
INTERNATIONAL, MALAYSIAN $$

22  Map p64, D2

From its clever name and slick design to its tasty twists on comfort foods, such as deep-fried Hainanese meatloaf sandwich and dessert toasties, LOKL ticks all the right boxes. This is also one of the few places in Chinatown to get a Western breakfast (8am to 11am). It's not obvious but there's an internal courtyard with outdoor seating at the back. (www.loklcoffee.com; 30 Jln Tun H S Lee; mains RM15-22; ⏱8am-8pm Tue-Sun; 📶; 🚇Masjid Jamek)

## Precious Old China
MALAYSIAN, NONYA $$

23  Map p64, B4

Run by the owners of Old China Café, this restaurant inside Central Market has an upscale, Shangai-1930s look, with lacquered chairs and pricey porcelain on display, but serves similar excellent Southeast Asian and Nonya dishes. Try the bitter gourd soup for something different. The restaurant also functions as a bar if you just want a drink. (📞2273 7372; www.oldchina.com.my; Mezzanine fl, Central Market, Jln Hang Kasturi; dishes RM8-23; ⏱11am-late; 🚇Pasar Seni)

---

## Local Life
## Breakfast in Chinatown

Breakfast on mainland China can be dreadful, but in KL's Cantonese-heavy Chinatown, it's a treat. Just off Petaling St on Jln Hang Lekir, in the heart of the pedestrian area, are two stalls that have been soothing early-morning appetites for decades. Chee Cheong Fun Stall (p72) serves melt-in-the-mouth *chee cheong fun* (rice noodles) doused with sweet and spicy sauces and a sprinkle of sesame seeds. A few metres down is the equally good Cantonese congee (rice porridge) stall **Hon Kee** (Map p64, C5; 93 Jln Hang Lekir; congee RM5; ⏱4.30am-3pm; 🚇Kota Raya). Frog-leg congee is its specialty.

# Drinking

## Omakase + Appreciate

COCKTAIL BAR

24  Map p64, D1

This cosy, retro cocktail bar is one of KL's top secret drinking spots. Sip sophisticated concoctions such as an Earl Grey Mar-tea-ni. Part of the fun is finding the entrance: look for the sign saying 'no admittance'. (www.facebook.com/OmakaseAppreciate; Basement, Bangunan Ming Annexe, 9 Jln Ampang; ⏰5pm-1am Tue-Fri, 9pm-1am Sat; 🛜; 🚇Masjid Jamek)

**Top Tip**

### Chinatown Bars

There are a couple of more formal bars in Chinatown, but most visitors prefer to sink cold beers at the open-air restaurants around Petaling Street Market (p79). Some of the backpacker digs have bars open to the public, including **Reggae Mansion** (Map p64, C5; ☎03-2072 6877; www.reggaehostelsmalaysia.com/mansion; 49-59 Jln Tun HS Lee; ❄@🛜; 🚇Masjid Jamek), which runs the open-air Rooftop Skybar. Precious Old China (p73) in Central Market also functions as a bar and is open till late. Drinking in public is not illegal, but it's best to avoid offence to Muslim sensibilities by not drinking in Merdeka Square or other public areas.

## Reggae Bar

BAR

25  Map p64, C5

Travellers gather in droves at this pumping bar in the thick of Chinatown, which has outdoor seats if you'd like to catch the passing parade. There are beer promos, pool tables and pub grub served till late. (www.reggaebarkl.com; 158 Jln Tun HS Lee; ⏰11.30am-late; 🚇Pasar Seni)

## Aku Cafe & Gallery

CAFE

26  Map p64, C6

Set in a long narrow shophouse that seems to go on forever, this relaxed coffee haunt serves good hand-drip brews starting at RM10. There are also flavoured drinks such as mint and lemon iced coffee, cakes, and light *kopitiam*-style meals. Exhibitions change on a monthly basis and there are some nice local craft souvenirs for sale. (☎2857 6887; www.facebook.com/akucafegallery; 1st fl, 8 Jln Panggong; ⏰11am-8pm Tue-Sun; 🛜; 🚇Pasir Seni)

## Moontree House

CAFE

27  Map p64, C6

This is a quiet space for a well-prepared hand-drip or syphon coffee in an old shophouse on the edge of Chinatown. Coffee beans are mostly directly sourced and include the local Johor-grown Liberica and Peabody Liberica. The latter makes for a sweet and slightly pungent ice-dripped

## Understand
# The Kapitan of Kuala Lumpur

- - - - - - - - - - - - - - - - - - - - - - - - - - - - - - - -

Few would deny the massive contribution Chinese immigrants have made to the development of KL. In the 19th century they came in large numbers to work the tin mines, and many became self-made tycoons within a very short time. Not surprisingly, the most successful have left their names across the city: from streets and buildings (Jln Tun HS Lee; Jln Yap Kwan Seng; Loke Mansion; Lee Rubber Building) to entire districts (Chow Kit) as well as various hospitals, schools and philanthropic societies.

The most famous Chinese immigrant to KL was undoubtedly Yap Ah Loy, the man now widely credited as the city's founder. He was 17 when he left his village in Guangdong, in southern China, in search of work in Malaya. Fifteen years later, in 1868, he had reached the highest position possible in the city's ethnic communities.

Yap began working life as a coolie, and soon his drive, fighting skills and talents with men made him assistant to the Kapitan Cina. The Kapitan post was created as a bridge between the colonial masters and the often unruly ethnic groups they governed. Elected by the community but appointed by the colonial government, they acted like governors and could enact laws and collect taxes.

When the current Kapitan Cina, Liu Ngim Kong, died in 1868, Yap was appointed as his successor. Through his control of the tin trade, as well as opium trading and prostitution, which thrived in the mining boomtown, he became exceptionally wealthy. It is estimated that in 1880 he owned 64 of the 200 houses in KL. This number only increased after he oversaw the rebuilding of KL (from wood and attap to the brick shophouses and arcades one sees today) after the great flood and fire in 1881.

When he died in 1885, Yap Ah Loy was the city's richest man, and so loved, feared and respected that government offices were closed on the day of his funeral. Today his name is found rather incongruously on the city's shortest street. More fittingly, he was canonised in 1956 by Sin Sze Si Ya Temple (p66), which he founded.

Today, you can visit Yap Ah Loy's grave in the sprawling Kwong Tong Cemetery (p119) south of the Royal Museum.

coffee. The shop also sells cute handicrafts and feminist literature.

(www.moontree-house.blogspot.com; 1st fl, 6 Jln Panggong; ⏱10am-8pm Wed-Mon; 🛜; 🚇Pasar Seni)

### Koong Woh Tong

TEAHOUSE

28  Map p64, C4

This little herbal drink shop is part of a Chinese chain that has spread into Southeast Asia. It sits at the northern mouth of Petaling Street Market, resplendent with its golden interior, and sells refreshing traditional herbal drinks. Try the musky Lou Kat or the refreshing Five Flower drink.

(cnr Jln Petaling & Jln Tun Tan Cheong Lock; 🚇Pasar Seni)

**Local Life**

### Chin Woo Stadium

This historic sports **stadium** (Map p64, D6; 📞2072 4602; www.chinwoo. org.my/en/home.php; Jln Hang Jebat; swimming adult/child RM5/2; ⏱2-8pm Mon-Fri, 9am-8pm Sat & Sun; 🚇Pasar Seni) sits atop a hill overlooking Chinatown. The highlight here is its 50m outdoor pool. If you're keen for a dip, note that all swimsuits must be tight-fitting, ie no baggy shorts even with an inner mesh lining, and you need a swimming cap as well. In the stadium itself various yoga classes are held every Monday at 7.30pm and there are badminton courts (racquets can be hired).

# Entertainment

### Kelantan Shadow Puppet Play

PUPPET THEATRE

29  Map p64, A3

There are daily live performances of Kelantan's brilliant *wayang kulit* (shadow puppetry) here. Kelantan is a centre for this folk art in which stories of the *Ramayana* epic are retold with accompanying music. However, performances in that state have been banned for decades under the conservative government, which considers it haram (sinful) because of its non-Islamic roots.

Located in the underground mall at Merdeka Square (buy tickets at KL City Gallery).

(📞012-321 5937; www.beringinemas.com; 70 Plaza Dataran Merdeka; tickets RM30; ⏱3pm daily; 🚇Masjid Jamek)

### Panggung Bandaraya

THEATRE

30  Map p64, B1

Originally designed as City Hall by famed British colonial architect AB Hubback, this handsome 1896 building with distinctive black domes has been refitted into one of KL's most beautiful theatrical spaces. The intimate auditorium's design is based on the shape of a Malaysian kite. Check with Visit KL (p150) for the latest shows.

(DBKL City Theatre; Jln Tun Perak; 🚇Masjid Jamek)

Panggung Bandaraya

## Petaling Street Art House

LIVE PERFORMANCE

31 ⭐ Map p64, D5

This intimate shophouse-based venue is keeping tradition alive in Chinatown with live performances of opera (Cantonese, Teochow and Hokkien varieties), puppetry, folk-music concerts and movies. Most events are in Chinese but don't let that stop you from attending. Check its Facebook page for upcoming events (ideally with a translating app).

(📞3326 2295; www.facebook.com/petaling-street.arthouse; 55 1A Jln Sultan; 🚇Pasar Seni)

## Muzium Musik

LIVE MUSIC

32 ⭐ Map p64, A3

This new museum of Malaysian music was about to open at press time and promised live performances as well as exhibits on the history and variety of traditional music. The building itself is one of the most striking around Merdeka Square (it was formerly the Chartered Bank Building, built in 1891).

(Jln Raja, Merdeka Sq; 🚇Masjid Jamek)

# Shopping

## Central Market
ARTS, CRAFTS

33 🔒 Map p64, B4

This 1930s art deco building houses dozens of shops selling Malaysian arts and crafts including batik clothing and hangings, *songket* (fine cloth woven with silver and gold thread), *wau bulan* (moon kites), baskets, Royal Selangor pewter and Nonya ceramics (real and good reproductions), as well as vintage items from daily life. You can often bargain the price down 10% to 20%.
(www.centralmarket.com.my; Jln Hang Kasturi; ☺10am-10pm; 🚇Pasar Seni)

### KL Academy of Traditional Chinese Medicine

In 1997 a collective of second-generation Chinatown pharmacists started the **KL Academy of Traditional Chinese Medicine** (Map p64, D7; 📞2026 5273; www.klatcm.weebly.com; 138-140 Jln Petaling; ☺6.30pm-10pm Mon-Fri, 2.30-9pm Sat, 9am-5pm Sun; 🚇Pasar Seni) to provide training for those wanting to learn the practices of traditional Chinese medicine. It offers a year-long course and operates as a drop-in clinic for patients.

## Peter Hoe Beyond
ARTS, CRAFTS

34 🔒 Map p64, C5

On the 2nd floor of the historic Lee Rubber Building, Peter Hoe's charming emporium fills nearly 900 sq metres with all manner of original fabric products such as tablecloths, curtains and robes (many hand-printed in India directly for Peter Hoe), as well as woven baskets, hanging lanterns, embroidered cushions, silverware, candles, and knick-knacks galore. A KL institution.
(📞2026 9788; 2nd fl, Lee Rubber Bldg, 145 Jln Tun HS Lee; ☺10am-7pm; 🚇Pasar Seni)

## Junk Bookstore
BOOKS

35 🔒 Map p64, C3

One of KL's best secondhand bookstores, with thousands of titles piled high on a couple of jam-packed floors. Ask staff to show you their selection of antique local titles, but don't expect to get them for bargain prices! Bring a mask if you suffer from allergies.
(📞2078 3822; 78 Jln Tun HS Lee; ☺8.30am-5pm Mon-Fri, 8.30am-2pm Sat; 🚇Masjid Jamek)

## House of Rinpo
ANTIQUES

36 🔒 Map p64, A3

In the underground mall at the southern end of Merdeka Square, this small antique shop is run as a hobby by affable Uncle Khoo. The quality of items varies but there are usually some good finds to be had among the ceramics, paintings, and daily life items from the past (we found a hand-painted kerosene lamp from the 1940s). (Plaza Dataran Merdeka; ⏱10am-6pm; 🚇Masjid Jamek)

### Purple Cane Tea Arts  TEA

37 🔒 Map p64, C6

One of several specialist tea shops in Chinatown where you can sample and buy Chinese teas (mostly *puer*), plus all the tea-making paraphernalia to go with them. (www.purplecane.com.my; 11 Jln Sultan; ⏱10am-7pm; 🚇Pasar Seni)

### Petaling Street Market  MARKET

38 🔒 Map p64, C5

Malaysia's relaxed attitude towards counterfeit goods is well illustrated at this heavily hyped night market bracketed by fake Chinese gateways. Traders start to fill Jln Petaling from midmorning until it is jam-packed with market stalls selling everything from fake Gucci handbags to bunches of lychees. Visit in the afternoon if you want to take pictures or see the market without the crowds. (Jln Petaling; ⏱noon-11pm; 🚇Kota Raya)

### Kwong Yik Seng  ARTS, CRAFTS

39 🔒 Map p64, C5

Looking for traditional Chinese teapots, bowls or a kitsch ornament for your mantlepiece? Your search is over at this shop specialising in new and antique-style china and porcelain. The Peranakan ware is not antique but

JOHN SONES SINGING BOWL MEDIA/GETTY IMAGES ©

Central Market

still pretty, and given its association with the Baba Nonya (descendants of mixed Malay and Chinese, also known as Peranakan) it's worth considering if you want a gift that's unique to Malaysia. (☎2078 3620; 144 Jln Tun HS Lee; ⏱9am-5pm Mon-Sat; 🚇Pasar Seni)

### Sang Kee  HANDICRAFTS

40 🔒 Map p64, C3

A rattan cane and bamboo shop in business since 1920. Most items come from China. (64 Jln Tun Perak; ⏱9am-3pm Mon-Fri; 🚇Masjid Jamek)

Explore

# Masjid India, Chow Kit & Kampung Baru

Sprawling over the northern part of KL, these distinct ethnic neighbourhoods attract visitors with their markets, traditional foods, and in the case of Kampung Baru (the 'new village'), their very existence. The village was reserved for Malays by the colonial administration in the 1890s, and for better and for worse, is still a charming throwback to earlier days.

# The Sights in a Day

Take the monorail to **Lake Titi-wangsa** (p85), a popular spot for strolling and snapping pics of the city's skyline. Visit the nearby **National Visual Arts Gallery** (p85) to get the latest on contemporary Malaysian art, and check if there are any interesting shows worth taking in at **Istana Budaya** (p91) that night.

Head back into town for lunch at **Yut Kee** (p90), a Hainanese *kopitiam* (coffee shop) that has been around since 1928. Then take a taxi to **Bank Negara Malaysia Museum & Art Gallery** (p84). There's a collection of small galleries here that offer a very informative and visual take on money, including how Islamic banking works. Afterwards, head to **Chow Kit** (p88) and slowly make your way to Kampung Baru. If it's Tuesday, Thursday or Sunday take the 2½-hour **walking tour** (p84); otherwise follow ours (p124).

You'll have plenty of chances for snacking in the village, but save your appetite for dinner at the **Coliseum Cafe** (p90), once a favourite haunt of Somerset Maugham. This is also one of few places to get a beer in the area. Next door are action-packed Indian movies at the **Coliseum Theatre** (p91), or head back into the Golden Triangle for nightlife.

 **Best of Kuala Lumpur**

**Street Food & Food Courts**
Kin Kin (p88)

Yut Kee (p90)

Capital Café (p89)

**Entertainment**
Sutra Dance Theatre (p91)

Istana Budaya (p91)

**Museums & Galleries**
Bank Negara Malaysia Museum & Art Gallery (p84)

National Visual Arts Gallery (p85)

**Green Spaces**
Lake Titiwangsa (p85)

**Heritage Buildings**
Loke Mansion (p86)

## Getting There

**LRT** Masjid Jamek for Masjid India area. Kampung Baru station for the southern edge of the village.

**Monorail** Chow Kit for Chow Kit Market and the northern edge of Kampung Baru. Titiwangsa station for Lake Titiwangsa.

**Taxi** For the Bank Negara museum.

Titwangsa Lake Gardens

Jln Pembeling

TITIWANGSA

Titiwangsa Lake Gardens

3

Lake Titiwangsa

National Visual Arts Gallery

4

Jln Tenteram

TITIWANGSA

Jln Raja Muda Abdul Aziz

Jln Haji Yahya Sheik Ahmad

Jln Hamzah

Jln Raja Uda

Jln Daud

11

21

Jln Tun Razak

Jln Kuantan

20

Persiaran Titiwangsa 3

Hospital Kuala Lumpur

Jln Raja Uda

Jln Pahang

Chow Kit Monorail

Jln Haji Hussein

Jln Pahang

CHOW KIT

Titiwangsa Monorail

Titiwangsa LRT

Jln Tun Razak

Sungai Gombak

Jln Ipoh

Jln Chow Kit

500 m

0.25 miles

**For reviews see**

| | | |
|---|---|---|
| ⊙ Sights | p84 |
| ✗ Eating | p88 |
| ✪ Entertainment | p91 |

PWTC LRT

Jln Ipoh

Jln Putra

Sungai Batu

Putra KTM

N

KAMPUNG
BARU

Jln Raja Muda Musa

Former
Sunday
Market
Kampung
Baru

Kampung Baru
1 Walking Tour

Kampung
Baru LRT

14

Muslim
Cemetery

Sungai Klang

Jln Ampang

6  Masjid Jamek
Kampung Baru

15

AKLEH (E12)

Bukit Nanas
Monorail

Jln Punchak

Jln Punchak

Jln P Ramlee

KL Forest
Eco Park

Jln Raja Alang

Sultan
Sulaiman
Club 5

Jln Raja Abdullah

Jln Sultan Ismail

Dang
Wangi
LRT

7

Tatt Khalsa
Diwan
Gurdwara

Jln D Sulaiman

10

Medan
Tuanku
Monorail

17

Jln Doraisamy

Jln Bukit Nanas

Jln Ampang

Jln Haji Taib

Jln Tunku Abdul Rahman (TAR)

Loke
Mansion

8

Jln Medan Tuanku

Jln Munshi Abdullah

18

Jln Tiong Nam

Sultan
Ismail
LRT

Jln Raja Laut

Jln Dang Wangi

13

Bandaraya
LRT

Lg TAR

Night
Market

16

Le TAR

Jln Masjid India

12
19

9

Masjid
India

22

Jln Raja Laut

Sungai Gombak

Jln Kuching

Jln Dato Onn

Jln Kuching

2

Bank Negara
Malaysia Museum
& Art Gallery

5

6

7

8

E

D

C

B

A

# Sights

## Kampung Baru Walking Tour
WALKING TOUR

1 ◉ Map p82, D5

The latest walking tour from Visit KL takes you into the heart of the traditonal Malay village at the centre of the city. The tour covers not only the sites, such as the Masjid Jamek (mosque), Sultan Sulaiman Club and the beautiful old wood houses, but also traditional shops, popular dishes and food venues, and teaches basic Malay customs. Dress conservatively and bring an umbrella. If you can't do the tour, download the informative PDF from the website. (☑2698 0332; www.visitkl.gov.my/visitklv2; ⊙4.30-7pm Tue, Thu & Sun)

## Bank Negara Malaysia Museum & Art Gallery
MUSEUM

2 ◉ Map p82, A7

This well-designed complex of small museums focuses on banking, finance and money and is not dull in the least. Highlights include a collection of ancient coins and money (and a slick interactive screen to examine their history), a gallery of the bank's private art collection, a surreal 3m-long tunnel lined with RM1 million (in the Children's Gallery), and a history of the little-known Islamic banking system (which must comply with sharia law, including prohibitions against usury). (www.museum.bnm.gov.my; Sasana Kijang, 2 Jln Dato Onn; admission free; ⊙10am-6pm; 🚇Bank Negara, then taxi)

---

### Understand

## Bumiputra Privileges

When the New Economic Policy (NEP) was introduced in 1971 its aim was that 30% of Malaysia's corporate wealth be in the hands of indigenous Malays, or *bumiputra* ('princes of the land'), within 20 years. A massive campaign of positive discrimination began, which handed majority control over the army, police, civil service and government to Malays. By 1990 a new Malay middle class had emerged; however, cronyism and discrimination against Indians and Chinese also increased.

Affirmative action programs continue to this day (under the NEP successor the National Development Policy), and according to the World Bank, these policies are a significant cause of migration out of Malaysia, especially of highly skilled workers. For travellers to KL, it is hard not to note the lack of Chinese and Indians working in banks and government institutions. The segregated education system has also led to a noticeable deterioration in English skills among younger Malays, but also ethnic Chinese who now tend to focus on Mandarin instruction.

Traditional Malay house, Kampung Baru

## Lake Titiwangsa

LAKE

3 ⊙ Map p82, E1

For a postcard-perfect view of the city skyline head to Lake Titiwangsa and the relaxing treed park that surrounds it. If you're feeling energetic, hire a row boat, go for a jog, play some tennis, or explore the nearby neighbourhood of handsome bungalows. The park is a favourite spot for courting Malaysian couples and about a 10-minute walk east of the monorail station.

(Taman Tasik Titiwangsa; monorail Titiwangsa)

## National Visual Arts Gallery

GALLERY

4 ⊙ Map p82, E2

Occupying a pyramid-shaped block, the NVAG showcases modern and contemporary Malaysian art. There are often interesting temporary shows of local and regional artists, as well as pieces from the gallery's permanent collection of 4000 pieces, including paintings by Zulkifi Moh'd Dohalan, Wong Hoi Cheong, Ahad Osman and the renowned batik artist Chuah Than Teng. Overall, though, the gallery lacks a wow factor.

(Balai Seni Lukis Negara; ☏ 4026 7000; www.artgallery.gov.my; 2 Jln Temerloh; admission free; ⊙ 10am-6pm; monorail Titiwangsa)

### Sultan Sulaiman Club

HISTORIC BUILDING

5  Map p82, D5

Dating back to 1901 (some sources say 1909), this is the oldest Malay club in KL and said to be where the meetings took place that led to the United Malays National Organisation (UMNO; the lead party in the ruling coalition). The original club building was demolished in the late '60s. In 2007 a local architectural firm constructed an exact replica, which is located across from the new club at the back of a field.

(Bangunan Warisan Kelab Sultan Suleiman; Jln Datuk Abdul Razak; 🚇Kampung Baru)

### Masjid Jamek Kampung Baru

MOSQUE

6  Map p82, D5

Though founded in the late 1880s, the present mosque structure dates back to the 1950s. This is Kampung Baru's principal mosque. It sports a handsome gateway decorated with eye-catching tiles in traditional Islamic patterns. Stalls around the mosque sell religious paraphernalia, including white *kopia* and black *songkok*, the traditional head coverings for Malay Muslim men. Outside the mosque look for the map that shows the seven smaller villages that make up Kampung Baru.

(Jln Raja Alang; 🚇Kampung Baru)

### Tatt Khalsa Diwan Gurdwara

SIKH TEMPLE

7  Map p82, C5

This is the largest Sikh temple in Southeast Asia, and spiritual home of KL's 75,000 Sikhs. There's been a temple and school here since 1924, though the present building dates from the 1990s. Visitors can enter and see the main shrine with a guide but must wear a headscarf (head wrap for men, which will be provided at the entrance) and pants or long dress. There's a free vegetarian lunch on Sundays open to all visitors.

(24 Jln Raja Alang; monorail Chow Kit)

### Loke Mansion

HISTORIC BUILDING

8  Map p82, C6

Rescued from the brink of dereliction by the law firm Cheang & Ariff, Loke Mansion was once the home of self-made tin tycoon Loke Yew. The Japanese high command also set up base here in 1942. After years of neglect, the mansion has been beautifully restored; access to the interior is by appointment only, but you're welcome

☑ Top Tip
**Ramadan in the Village**

Kampung Baru is a great area to visit during Ramadan, when street markets offer delicacies prepared specially to break the daily fast. The Ramadan Street Bazaar runs along Jln Raja Alang and Jln Raja Muda Musa between 4pm and 8pm daily. Among the delicacies to try are *bubur lambuk* (rice porridge).

## Understand

# Kampung Baru

A *kampung* is a village, and in Kuala Lumpur, which still has a number of urban *kampungs*, there is none so famous as Kampung Baru, literally the 'new village'. In the shadow of the Petronas Towers across the Klang River, this Malay stronghold is still largely a community of wood houses, food courts, traditional shops, and a place where children and chickens can run free.

As its name suggests, Kampung Baru is not terribly old. In the late 1890s the British authorities, worried about the declining number of Malay residents in the capital, gazetted 89.4 hectares as a Malay Agricultural Settlement, and in 1900 relocated Malays from the Masjid Jamek area.

The first census in 1928 showed there were 544 households and 2600 villagers. The Malays themselves divided their numbers into seven villages, according to ancestral origins, which included Malacca and Java. Intervillage marriage, and even play among children, was restricted.

Kampung Baru saw the first Malay club develop, and it played a positive role in the anti-colonial protests that led to independence. By the 1960s, however, it was falling behind the rest of the city. Resentment over this is said to have contributed to the village being a centre for violence during the 1969 race riots (which pitted Malays against the more prosperous Chinese).

In the coming decades Kampung Baru also became physically separated from the rest of the city, as dike walls, and later the Petronas Towers and LRT construction, left it a near orphan on the wrong side of the river. Even today it is a startling shift to go one LRT stop from KLCC to Kampung Baru.

Revitalisation of the village is always said to be around the corner, but when it really comes, it won't be easy. Two administrations and competing laws govern the small slice of land, and property titles are incredibly complex: there are an estimated 4200 beneficiaries across 880 separate lots. In 2011 the Kampung Baru Development Corporation was formed, with the promise that this time things would be different. In late 2014 the Sunday Market grounds were razed, a sign that perhaps change is truly coming to this pocket of KL stuck in time.

anytime to pause in the driveway and admire the whitewashed exterior. (☎2691 0803; 273A Jln Medan Tuanku; ⊙9am-5pm Mon-Fri; monorail Medan Tuanku)

## Masjid India                    MOSQUE

9  ◎  Map p82, B8

The original wooden mosque that gives the area its name, Masjid India was built in 1883 but replaced by a bulky red granite tiled modern structure in 1963. It's not much to look at, and you can't go inside, but it's fronted by a busy market and surrounded by stalls selling religious

### Local Life
### Multicultural Markets
On Saturday nights in Masjid India look for the **Pasar Malam** (Night Market; Map p82, B8; Lg Tuanku Abdul Rahman; ⊙3pm-midnight Sat; 🚇Masjid Jamek). Among the sari and scarf stalls, hawkers sell excellent Chinese, Malay and Indian snacks and drinks.

**Bazaar Baru Chow Kit** (Chow Kit Market; Map p82, C5; 469-473 Jln TAR; ⊙8am-5pm; monorailChow Kit) is a daily wet and sundry market serving the Chinese and Malay working class of Chow Kit. You can sample hawker and *kopitiam* (coffee shop) food and drinks.

Kampung Baru was known for its Saturday/Sunday *pasar minggu*, a mostly Malay affair, but in 2014 the market area was razed. Tourism officials expect vendors will return at some point at a different location.

items and traditional Malay costumes. The area's famous Saturday *pasar malam* (night market) runs along Lg TAR behind the mosque. (http://masjidindia.com; Jln Masjid India; 🚇Masjid Jamek)

# Eating

## Kin Kin                    CHINESE $

10  🍴  Map p82, C6

Everyone in KL knows this bare-bones shop and the famous dish it serves: chilli *pan mee*. These 'dry' noodles, topped with a soft boiled egg, minced pork, *ikan bilis* (small, deep-fried anchovies), fried onion and a special spicy chilli sauce, are one of the city's taste sensations. If you don't eat pork, staff do a version topped with mushrooms. (40 Jln Dewan Sultan Sulaiman; noodles RM7; ⊙7.30am-9pm Mon-Fri, 7.30am-4pm Sat & Sun; monorail Medan Tuanku)

## D'Istana Jalamas Café                    MALAYSIAN $

11  🍴  Map p82, D2

The cafe at Istana Budaya (the national theatre) offers a serve-yourself buffet of Malay and *mamak* (Muslim-Malay) favourites such as fish-head curry, as well as salads, snacks and fresh fruit. Try the local coffee: it's filtered here and not simply a powdered mix. Balcony seats overlook nearby Titiwangsa Park. (Jln Tun Razak, Lake Titiwangsa; mains RM5-10; ⊙7am-8pm Mon-Fri; monorail Titiwangsa)

Pasar Malam night market

## Masjid India Hawker Court
HAWKER $

**12** ✕ Map p82, C8

A bustling covered hawker court serving all the usual Malay, Indian and Chinese favourites. Good to visit if you can't make it to the Saturday *pasar malam*. (Jln Masjid India; dishes RM2-10; ⊘8am-9pm; 🚇Masjid Jamek)

## Capital Café
MALAY $

**13** ✕ Map p82, B7

Since it opened in 1956 this truly Malaysian cafe has had Chinese, Malays and Indians all working together in the same space. Try its excellent *mee goreng* or *rojak* (salad doused in a peanut-sauce dressing) or satay (only available in the evenings). (213 Jln TAR; dishes RM4-6; ⊘10am-8pm Mon-Sat; 🚇Bandaraya)

## Kak Som
MALAYSIAN $

**14** ✕ Map p82, D5

Specialising in east coast Peninsular Malaysian dishes such as *nasi kerabu* (blue rice), this is a good place to dine inexpensively on the main Kampung Baru restaurant strip. Take your pick of items from the buffet along with rice, sit down and the waitstaff will come to take a drink order and tally up your bill. (Jln Raja Muda Musa; meals RM7; ⊘8am-3am; 🚇Kampung Baru)

Top Tip

## Pusaka: Revealing & Preserving Tradition

Check the Facebook page of NGO **Pusaka** (www.facebook.com/pages/Pusaka/161861580538209), which means 'tradition', to get updates on traditional art events around Kuala Lumpur. The group has been working for years to keep Malaysian arts alive by both introducing them to the general public, and by training a new generation in such forms as *wayang kulit* (shadow puppetry), *mak yong* (dance-theatre) and also various Chinese performing arts. Shows are by donation and often feature some outstanding older performers and the occasional young phenom.

Other arts groups to follow are **Kakiseni** (www.facebook.com/mykakiseni), **Daily Seni** (www.facebook.com/DailySeni) and **MapKl** (www.facebook.com/mapkl).

## Ikan Bakar Berempah      HAWKER $

15  Map p82, D5

This excellent barbecued-fish stall sits within a hawker-stall market covered by a zinc roof. Pick your fish off the grill and add *kampung*-style side dishes to it off the long buffet. (Jln Raja Muda Musa; meals RM5-10; ⏲7am-12.30pm & 5-10pm; 🚇Kampung Baru)

## Coliseum Cafe      INTERNATIONAL $$

16 🍴 Map p82, B8

Little seems to have changed here since Somerset Maugham tucked into its famous sizzling steaks and Hainan Chicken Chops. Opened in 1921, the cafe is Malaysia's longest-running Western restaurant. Though far less polished than the Majestic Hotel, it's much more locally loved, and the food truly hits the spot. (📞2692 6270; 100 Jln TAR; dishes RM13-49, weekday set lunches RM24-29; ⏲10am-10pm; 🚇Masjid Jamek)

## Yut Kee      CHINESE, WESTERN $$

17 🍴 Map p82, C7

In 2014 this beloved Hainanese *kopitiam*, in business since 1928, was forced to move round the corner to its present location. With much of the old furnishings the same, the new shop is a reasonable facsimile, and the food hasn't changed: try the chicken chop, *roti babi* (French toast stuffed with pork), toast with homemade *kaya* (coconut-cream jam), or Hokkien mee. (📞2698 8108; 1 Jln Kamunting; meals RM6-15; ⏲8am-5pm Tue-Sun; 🚇Dang Wangi)

## Mungo Jerry      CHINESE $$

18 🍴 Map p82, B5

This late-night supper hot spot on the edge of Chow Kit is a bare-bones joint famous for its chilli-infused pork curry stew, *bak kut teh*, as well as the original more soupy version. Locals will tell you the quality has dropped in recent years as the original owner has left the cooking to his helpers, but you are unlikely to notice.

(292 Jln Raja Laut; dishes RM8-12; ⏱5pm-2.30am; 🚇Sultan Ismail)

## Saravanaa Bhavan INDIAN $$

 19 Map p82, C8

This global chain of restaurants offers some of the best-quality Indian food you'll find in KL. Their banana-leaf and mini-tiffin feasts are supremely tasty and you can also sample southern Indian classics such as *masala dosa* (rice-and-lentil- crepe stuffed with spiced potatoes).

(📞2698 3293; www.saravanabhavan.com; 52 Jln Maarof, Bangsar; meals RM10-20; ⏱8am-11pm; 🍴; 🚇Masjid Jamek)

# Entertainment

## Sutra Dance Theatre DANCE

 20 ⭐ Map p82, D1

The home of Malaysian dance legend Ramli Ibrahim, who once again wowed New York on tour in 2014, has been turned into a showcase for Indian classical dance as well as a dance studio, painting and photography gallery and cultural centre near Lake Titiwangsa. See its website for upcoming events.

(www.sutrafoundation.org.my; 12 Persiaran Titiwangsa 3, Titiwangsa; monorail Titiwangsa)

 Local Life

## Semua House Wedding Shop

Two floors of Indian wedding shops can be found at this **department store** (Map p82, B8; cnr Jln Masjid India & Jln Bunus 6; ⏱10am-10pm; 🚇Masjid Jamek), right in the heart of Masjid Jamek. The perfume selection at the entrance is particularly impressive.

## Istana Budaya PERFORMING ARTS

21 ⭐ Map p82, D2

Big-scale drama and dance shows are staged here, as well as music performances by the National Symphony Orchestra and National Choir. The building's soaring roof is based on a traditional Malay floral decoration of betel leaves, while the columned interior invokes a provincial colonialism. There's a dress code of no shorts, and no short-sleeved shirts.

(National Theatre; 📞4026 5555; www.istanabudaya.gov.my; Jln Tun Razak, Titiwangsa; tickets RM100-300; monorail Titiwangsa)

## Coliseum Theatre CINEMA

22 ⭐ Map p82, B8

One of KL's oldest still-functioning cinemas, this art deco-style building dates back to 1920 and screens Indian-language movies.

(94 Jln TAR; 🚇Masjid Jamek)

## Local Life
# Ampang Amble

**Getting There**

Ampang runs east of KLCC until you get to the eastern foothills.

**Taxi** The best way to get anywhere in Ampang is by taxi or walking.

The tin mining that fuelled KL's rise in the 19th century began here in Ampang and continued till the early 1980s. These days dredging sites have become lake parks, and the general area is one of the city's leafier – and wealthier – suburbs, a great place for strolling, admiring eclectic post-war bungalows, and dining and shopping at some of the city's best off-the-tourist-track venues.

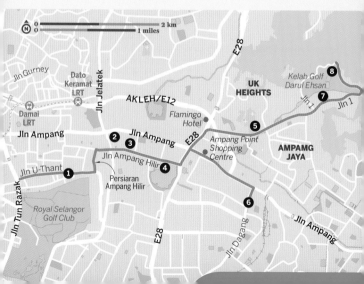

## ❶ Jalan U-Thant & Jalan Ampang Hilir

Start at the intersection of Jln U-Thant and Jln Tun Razak. Jln U-Thant, one of KL's most charming roads, is canopied with massive rain and banyan trees, and dotted with handsome bungalows. Make your way up to Jln Ampang Hilir, another lovely road, until you reach the back of Great Eastern Mall.

## ❷ Great Eastern Mall

This upscale **mall** (www.greateasternmall. com.my; 303 Jln Ampang; ⏰10am-10pm; 🚇Ampang Park) has **Ang Eng**, a custom-made *kebaya* shop, and shoemaker **Thomas Chan**. More surprising is **Alexis Ampang**, (📞4260 2288; www.alexis. com.my; Ground fl, Great Eastern Mall, 303 Jln Ampang; 🚇Ampang Park), a bistro by day, and weekend nights one of the city's top venues for live jazz music.

## ❸ My Batik Visitor Centre

Founded by artist Emilia Tan and set in a leafy compound, **My Batik** (📞016 220 3190; www.mybatik.org.my; 333 Persiaran Ritchie, off Jln Ritchie; ⏰8am-5pm; 🚇Ampang Park, then taxi) sells colourful batik print fashions and offers demonstration sessions and DIY classes for adults and children. The **Green Tomato Cafe** (www. facebook.com/greentomatocafe.com.my; 333 Persiaran Ritchie, off Jln Ritchie; breakfast RM15-18; ⏰8am-5pm) in the same compound serves all-day Western breakfast.

## ❹ Taman Tasik

Giant trees continue to form a canopy as you head to Taman Tasik. The park

has a pretty lake formed as a result of the tin mining that made KL rich (Ampang means 'dam'). Stop for a stroll and a *rojak*, a traditional fruit dish.

## ❺ Zaini Satay

The traffic-snarled walk to this **satay stand** (Naan Corner, Jln Kerja Ayer Lama; satay RM.80-1.20; ⏰6pm-midnight; 🚇Ampang Park, then taxi) in a food court in front of a 7-Eleven is worth it because the grandson of the 1960s King of Satay knows his business. This is likely the best satay you'll find in KL.

## ❻ Jalan Dagang

If you want to make a local smile, eat a durian. In season (June to August and usually again in December), make a detour to Jln Dagang, one of the top spots for fresh durian sold roadside. Musang King, a durian variety, has a creamy texture like custard.

## ❼ Taman TAR

A late-afternoon stroll around Taman TAR on Jln 1 is a treat. You'll be accompanied by happy locals breathing deep the fresh air coming off the jungle. The loop takes 40 minutes; round the north side of the golf course you'll often see troops of macaque and leaf monkeys.

## ❽ Tamarind Springs

One of KL's best secret restaurants is this open-air Indo-Chinese **venue** (📞4256 9300; Jln 1, Taman TAR, Selangor; dishes RM30-90; ⏰noon-3pm & 6.30-11.30pm) set in the jungle.

## Top Sights
# Batu Caves

### Getting There

Batu Caves are 13km north of KL central.

🚕 **Taxi** Taxi from KL is easiest.

🚉 **Train** KTM Komuter train to Batu Caves.

One of Malaysia's national treasures, and holiest Hindu sites, this complex of giant limestone caves houses temples that have been drawing pilgrims for more than 120 years. The American naturalist William Hornaday is credited with discovering the caves in 1878, though they were already known to Chinese settlers and of course to the local indigenous peoples. The caves are always an atmospheric, colourful (some might say joyfully tacky) and fascinating place to visit and no more so than in late January or early February when one million pilgrims converge during the three-day Thaipusam festival.

# Don't Miss

### Temple Cave

In 1891, K Thambusamy Pillai, founder of the Sri Mahamariamman Temple in KL, established a shrine to Lord Murugan at Batu Caves. At the foot of 272 steps leading up to the main dome-shaped cavern stands a 42.5m gaudy golden statue of Murugan, son of Shiva, and Hindu god of war. Inside the first cavern the lord's six abodes are carved into the walls, while a second cavern holds the temple of Valli Devanai, his wife. Prayer times are held at 8.30am and 4pm.

### Dark Cave

At step 204, branch off to the Dark Cave to follow a 45-minute **guided tour** (www.darkcavemalaysia.com; adult/child RM35/25; ☺10am-5pm Mon-Fri, 10am-5.30pm Sat & Sun) along 800m of the 2km of surveyed passageways within seven different chambers. Dramatic limestone formations including gorgeous flowstones, pits used for guano extraction, two species of bats and hundreds of other life forms, including the rare trapdoor spider, make this a fascinating excursion. Tours run every 20 minutes.

### Ramayana Cave

Perhaps no cave at Batu is more spectacularly over-embellished and enjoyable than the **Ramayana Cave** (admission RM2; ☺9am-5pm), which boasts gaudy dioramas of the Indian epic *Ramayana*. Near the entrance, look for the giant Gulliver-like statue of Kumbhakarna, brother of Ravana and a deep sleeper (he once snoozed for six months). Further up the narrow but towering cave interior, past two artificial flowing streams, is a shrine to a naturally occurring linga. This phallic-like stalagmite is a symbol of Shiva.

---

☏6189 6284

www.batucavesmuruga.org

Temple Cave free, entry fee for other caves

☺8am-8.30pm

## ☑ Top Tips

▸ Combine an afternoon visit to the caves with a morning exploration of the nearby Forestry Research Institute of Malaysia (FRIM; p96).

▸ Try to schedule a visit to include the Dark Cave tour to gain an understanding of the cave's rich natural history.

▸ If taking a taxi back to KL, look out for a dramatic ridge to the east. That's Tabur, reportedly the largest quartz ridgeline in the world.

## ✖ Take a Break

There is a block of restaurants on the right as you approach the stairs to Temple Cave. Try **Rani Vilas Restoran** (RM5-10; ☺7am-10pm) for excellent veggie thali sets, rotis and dosa.

## Top Sights
# Forestry Research Institute of Malaysia (FRIM)

FRIM is 16km northwest of KL.

🚕 **Taxi** direct from KL is best.

🚆 **Train** KTM Komuter train to Kepong Sentral then taxi.

Birdsong and wall-to-wall greenery replaces the drone of traffic at the Forestry Research Institute of Malaysia. Covering nearly 600 hectares, the institute was established in 1929 to research the sustainable management of Malaysia's rainforests. For visitors and locals, FRIM functions as a giant park, with quiet roads for cycling and well-established trails through the jungle landscape. There's a wide variety of flora and native wildlife to discover, from leaf monkeys and colourful birds to indigenous fruit trees and rare old dipterocarps.

Canopy walkway

## Don't Miss

### Canopy Walkway

The highlight of FRIM is this **canopy walkway** (adult/child RM10/1; ⏱9am-2.30pm, last trip 1.30pm, closed Mon & Fri), hanging a vertigo-inducing 30m above the forest floor. The 200m walkway takes you right into the canopy, offering great views of the rainforest with the towers of KL rising in the distance behind.

Heading down from the walkway the trail picks its way through the jungle (following the water pipe) to a shady picnic area, where you can cool off in a series of shallow waterfalls. The return hike incorporating the walkway takes about two hours. Bring water with you.

### Wooden Houses & Museum

At the far end of the soccer field, look for a couple of handsome traditional raised wooden houses built from hard cendol wood. Relocated from Malacca and Terenganu, the houses show regional variations such as in the use of roofing material (tile versus attap) and other features.

Drop by the **museum** (admission free; ⏱9am-noon & 2-4pm, closed Mon) near the information centre to learn more about the work of FRIM and the makeup of Malaysian forests.

### Hiking & Biking

The quiet roads circling the park are ideal for strolling, and when the forest is set back from an adjacent field they offer an intriguing look at the many layers of vegetation. Numerous clearly marked trails also run through the reserve. Bikes can be rented outside the park for RM5 to RM8 per hour. If you have time, consider extending your ride around the leafy neighbouring village of Kepong.

FRIM

☑6279 7592

www.frim.gov.my

adult/child RM5/1

⏱9am-7pm

### ☑ Top Tips

▶ Mornings are best at FRIM as the canopy walkway closes in the afternoon, when heavy rain showers are more common.

▶ Buy tickets for the canopy walkway (and pick up a park map) at the souvenir shop/ information centre. If no one is there, head directly up to the canopy walkway.

### ✗ Take a Break

There's a canteen and cafe within the park but opening hours are erratic. A couple of small restaurants sit outside the main gates but it's best to bring your own supplies.

Explore

# Lake Gardens & Brickfields

The colonialists may have built the green oasis of the Lake Gardens, but the Malaysians have put their mark on it with a new name, a bird park and a ring of excellent museums. Brickfields, by contrast, got its start as a place where – you guessed it – bricks were made, and today is a dense, vibrant Indian neighbourhood, rewarding for urban exploration and street-food sampling.

# The Sights in a Day

☼ Hit the **Royal Museum** (p104) when it opens at 9am – (ask your taxi driver to take you via **Kwong Tong Cemetery** (p105). After exploring the vast mansion head to the **National Museum** (p108), visit the lower floors, and then take a taxi to the **KL Bird Park** (p101). If you need lunch first, try its **Hornbill Restaurant** (p113).

☼ After a couple of hours with the birds, head across the street for a quick look at the **Orchid & Hibiscus Gardens** (p101). If you want to see Lake Perdana, catch the park's electric shuttle bus. Or go directly to the **Islamic Arts Museum** (p102) to tick off its highlights. When the museum closes at 5pm head to the **Old KL Train Station** (p108) to see one of KL's most iconic colonial buildings.

☾ For a fine meal in fine surroundings check into the **Colonial Cafe** (p115). Or head to Brickfields, KL's Little India, for vegetarian delights at **Annalakshmi** (p112); there's a good **gift shop** (p117) here too. Check if the **Temple of Fine Arts** (p116) is having a show. Otherwise, stroll around Brickfields; many **temples** (p111) and shrines are open until 9pm.

 **Top Sights**

Tun Abdul Razak Heritage Park (p100)

Royal Museum (p104)

Islamic Arts Museum (p102)

♥ **Best of Kuala Lumpur**

**Street Food & Food Courts**
Little India Fountain Stalls (p115)

**Museums & Galleries**
Islamic Arts Museum (p102)

National Museum (p108)

Royal Museum (p104)

**Green Spaces**
Tun Abdul Razak Heritage Park (p100)

Kwong Tong Cemetery (p105)

**Religious & Heritage Buildings**
Sree Veera Hanuman Temple (p111)

Masjid Negara (p110)

Old KL Train Station (p108)

## Getting There

**Monorail** KL Sentral or Tun Sambanthan for Brickfields.

🚈**LRT** KL Sentral for Brickfields.

🚃 **Train** KTM Komuter Train Kuala Lumpur station for Lake Gardens. KL Sentral for Brickfields.

🚌 **Bus** KL Hop-on Hop-off buses between destinations in and around Lake Gardens.

## Top Sights
# Tun Abdul Razak Heritage Park

This lush, 101-hectare landscaped park is better known, and more aptly described, by its colonial-era moniker: the Lake Gardens. This is KL's largest green space, and you can spend hours exploring the rolling terrain. The top sight is the sprawling Bird Park, but there are other worthies nearby, including two of KL's best museums connected by a stroll through flower gardens followed by tour along the lake.

Lake Gardens

⦿ Map p106, C3

www.visitkl.gov.my/visitklv2

🕑 7am-8pm

🚌 KL Hop-On, Hop-Off bus tour, 🚇 Kuala Lumpur

KL Bird Park

# Don't Miss

### KL Bird Park

This 21-acre **aviary** (📞03-2272 1010; www.klbirdpark.com; Jln Cenderawasih; adult/child RM48/38; 🕐9am-6pm; 🚇Kuala Lumpur) houses some 3000 birds representing 200 species of (mostly) Asian birds. The park is divided into four sections: in the first two birds fly freely beneath an enormous canopy. Section three features the native hornbills, while section four offers the less-edifying spectacle of caged species.

### Gardens

At the northern edge of the lake is the **Perdana Botanical Garden** (📞2617 6404; www.klbotanicalgarden.gov.my; admission free; 🕐7am-8pm; ♿; 🚇Kuala Lumpur) showcasing a wide variety of native and overseas plants, with sections dedicated to ferns, rare trees, medicinal herbs and so on.

Directly across from the Bird Park are the **Orchid & Hibiscus Gardens** (Taman Orkid (9am-6pm; admission Sat & Sun RM; Jln Cenderawasih; admission Sat & Sun RM1, Mon-Fri free; 🕐9am-6pm; 🚇Kuala Lumpur), that display hundreds of species of orchids and hibiscus, the latter Malaysia's national flower.

### Royal Malaysia Police Museum

One of KL's best small **museums** (5 Jln Perdana; admission free; 🕐9am-6pm Tue-Sun, closed 12.30-2.30pm Fri; 🚇Kuala Lumpur) offers a fascinating history of Malaysia through the story of policing. Discover not just the uniforms that distinguished British- from Dutch- from Sultan-era law enforcers, but also the crime issues that plagued them. The standout display, though, is the gallery of weapons, from handmade guns and knives to automatic weapons, hand grenades and swords, all seized from members of criminal 'secret societies' and communists during the Emergency.

## ☑ Top Tips

▶ Visit the Bird Park and gardens in the morning and museums in the afternoon to avoid being caught outdoors in the rain.

▶ The KL Hop-on Hop-off shuttle will get you to the Bird Park and lake. For transport around the park there is an electric shuttle (adult/child RM2/1) from 9am to 5pm.

▶ All the roads in the park are lined with wide sidewalks and there are many pedestrian-only trails.

## ✗ Take a Break

Head to the Bird Park's own Hornbill Restaurant (p113) for Western and Malay staples, best enjoyed (with the free flying fowl) on the wood deck overlooking the park. For something more local try the hawker stalls at Kompleks Makan Tanglin (p112).

## Top Sights
# Islamic Arts Museum

This striking-looking museum holds the largest collection of Islamic arts in Southeast Asia. If a museum can present an argument, this one presses that the rich heritage of Islam extends far beyond the Middle East. Hence, in addition to pieces from Iran, Syria and Turkey, you'll find entire sections devoted to Islamic art from China, India, and various Southeast Asian nations as well as themed displays on architecture, armour, coins, manuscripts, ceramics and more.

Muzium Kesenian Islam Malaysia

👁 Map p106, D3

☎ 2274 2020

www.iamm.org.my

Jln Lembah Perdana

adult/child RM14/7

🕐 10am-6pm

🚇 Kuala Lumpur

# Don't Miss

### Damascus Room

A Damascus Room is a style of winter reception chamber popular during the Ottoman period (1516–1918) in Syria's capital. The museum's stunning example was built in 1820. As is typical, the interior is composed of painted wood panels, and while it appears to be a single room it is actually divided into three sections marked by vaulted arches. There are so many details to admire here, from the ceiling woodwork, to the inlaid marble floor, to the inscribed poetry, to the *murqarnas* (stalactite wood features) of the wall niche.

### Kiswah

Kiswah is the large black embroidered cloth used to cover the holy Kaaba (the cubic building at the centre of the most holy mosque of Mecca). The museum has an entire Kiswah on display, a rare sight as they are usually cut and distributed to pilgrims after the hajj.

### Architecture Gallery

This popular gallery has scale models of important Islamic buildings including the Masjid al-Haram in Mecca (where the Kiswah-covered Kaaba sits), and the surviving traditional timber-framed mosques of Peninsular Malaysia. The latter were influenced by both Chinese and Indonesian architecture, as well as local vernacular styles, and look nothing like you expect of a mosque.

### Qur'an & Manuscript Gallery

Look for the 19th-century Qurans from Malaysia's east coast decorated in red, gold and black as well as the wide collection of miniature paintings, one of the few art forms in Islam that show the human face and figure.

## ☑ Top Tips

▶ Allow at least three hours to cover the museum exhibits.

▶ The gift shop has an excellent selection of books and some decorative arts.

▶ Plan to combine a visit here with a day in the park (p100) – so remember your umbrella.

▶ There is a pedestrian underpass near the National Museum connecting it to Perdana Lake. Walking from here to the Islamic Arts Museum via KL Bird Park takes about an hour.

## ✗ Take a Break

Just up the road at the KL Bird Park enjoy Malay or Western fare at the Hornbill Restaurant (p113). For maximum convenience, the museum has its own **restaurant** (set lunch RM52), but we find the atmosphere cold and the food mediocre.

## Top Sights
# Royal Museum

In 1928 Chinese tin tycoon Chan Wing built a mansion for his large family; it was later used as the residence of the Japanese Governor during KL's WWII occupation. In 1957 it became the National Palace, the residence of the king and queen of Malaysia. Finally, in 2011, with the opening of a new palace complex, the Royal Museum was born. After a restricted start, visitors are now permitted to tour the first two floors of the mansion, and wander the outside to take in the lush views

Muzium Diraja

Map p106, E6

Jln Istana

adult/child RM10/5

9am-5pm

Taxi

# Don't Miss

### The Decor

The palace exterior, with its eclectic European style, looks much the same as it was in Chan Wing's day. But the interior was obviously altered to suit both royal tastes and royal needs. There are major and minor waiting rooms, a small throne room (for royal events), an office for the king, a family room (including KTV), and a dozen or so bedrooms for guests and family alike. Floral wallpaper, upholstered furniture, thick carpets, crystal chandeliers and some gaudy posters reveal the *Downton Abbey*–meets-'70s-suburbia tastes of the royals, though Malay colours and motifs remind you where you are.

### The Dentist Room

You are sure to shudder when you see the royal dentist room, where family members were treated during weekly visits. Some visitors mistake this for a torture chamber when they first enter.

### Kwong Tong Cemetery

This fascinating cemetery lies directly south of the museum and is notable not just for its immense size (333 hectares of rolling grassy hills and fragrant frangipani trees) but the many notables buried within. These include Kapitan Yap Ah Loy, founder of KL. Chan Wing, the original owner of the Royal Museum building, is not buried here but his tin-mining partner, Cheong Yoke Choy, a noted philanthropist, is. There are also memorials to WWII dead. Pick up a map at the cemetery office.

## ☑ Top Tips

▶ At the time of press there was talk of implementing a dress code so be prepared with pants or a sarong.

▶ The Kwong Tong Cemetery lies south of the museum and can be visited on the way to or from Thean Hou Temple (p118).

## ✗ Take a Break

Though it's just behind the museum, it can be tricky to reach **Ikan Bakar Jalan Bellamy** (Map p106, E7; Jln Bellamy; meals RM10; ⊙11am-11pm Mon-Sat; monorail Tun Sambanthan), a group of barbecued-fish hawker stalls that the king himself sometimes ordered grilled stingray from. Try to sneak up the road behind the Royal Museum bathrooms rather than walking the big loop from the carpark.

Just a few minutes' taxi ride away you can enjoy a meal in another handsome pre-war building at the Colonial Cafe (p115).

Masjid Jamek LRT

MERDEKA SQUARE

Jln Raja Laut

Sungai Klang

Jln Kinabalu

Jln Sultan Hishamuddin

Jln Tun Tan Cheng Lock

Jln Kinabalu

Old KL Train Station

Kuala Lumpur

2

KTM 3

Headquarters Building

19 11

17

Majestic Spa

Masjid Negara 8

Jln Parlimen

13

Jln Cenderasari

KL Butterfly Park 5

Jln Lembah Perdana

Islamic Arts Museum

Jln Cender-awasih

15

Jln Perdana

Jln Perdana

LAKE GARDENS

Jln Tanbusu

Tun Abdul Razak Heritage Park

Tasik Perdana

Jln Cenderamulia

Jln Parlimen

Persiaran Mahameru

Jln Damansara

Jln Cenderamulia

Jln Sultan Salahuddin

Tun Abdul Razak Heritage Park (Lake Gardens)

20

Jln Istana

Royal
Museum

Jln Bellamy

Jln Syed Putra

Sri Kandaswamy
Temple 7

Sungai Klang

Jln Tebing

**For reviews see**

| | |
|---|---|
| Top Sights | p100 |
| Sights | p108 |
| Eating | p112 |
| Drinking | p115 |
| Entertainment | p116 |
| Shopping | p117 |

400 m

0        0.14 miles

Sree Veera
Hanuman
Temple

Jln Scott

9

12

23

Jln Tun Sambanthan

Jln Tun Sambanthan 3

Jln Padang Belia

Tun
Sambanthan
Monorail

22

BRICKFIELDS

Sam Kow Tong
Temple 10

KL
Sentral

18

24

14

KL Sentral
Monorail

Jln Tun Sambanthan 4

Jln Thambipillai

Jln Thambipillai

Vivekanandac
Ashram

6

Jln Rozario

Jln Sultan Abdul Samad

21

Hundred
Quarters 4

Jln Sultan Hishamuddin

National
Museum

1

Jln Travers

Lg Travers

Jln Bukit Travers

Jln Selangor

Jln Tun Sambanthan

Jln Travers

Jln Bangsar

16

Bangsar
LRT

Jln Syed Putra

5

6

7

8

A

B

C

D

E

# Sights

## National Museum

MUSEUM

1  Map p106, C5

Exhibit quality varies, but overall this museum offers a rich look at Malaysian history. The best exhibits are *Early History,* with artefacts from neolithic and Bronze Age cultures, and *The Malay Kingdoms,* which highlights the rise of Islamic kingdoms in the Malay Archipelago. Outside, look for a gorgeous traditional raised house; ancient burial poles from Sarawak; a regularly changing exhibition (extra charge); and two excellent small free side galleries, the **Orang Asli Craft Museum** and **Malay World Ethnology Museum**.
(Muzium Negara; 📞2282 6255; www.muzium negara.gov.my; Jln Damansara; adult/child RM5/2; ⊙9am-6pm; 🚌Hop-on-Hop-off bus tour, 🚇KL Sentral, then taxi)

### Local Life

### Sri Sakthi Vinayagar Temple

The original **shrine** (Map p106, C7; Jln Berhala) for Lord Vinayagar (the remover of obstacles) in Brickfields was a squatter shack on Jln Sultan Abdul Samad. Such was the humble start of many temples in this immigrant community. The current temple, reached via a short staircase, is still simple but has a tender devotional atmosphere, and inside one statue of Lord Vinayagar is made of bananas and brown sugar.

## Old KL Train Station

HISTORIC BUILDING

2  Map p106, E4

One of KL's most distinctive colonial buildings, this 1910 train station (replaced as a transit hub by KL Sentral in 2001) is a grand if ageing structure designed by British architect AB Hubback in the Mughal (or Indo-Saracenic) style. The building's walls are white plaster, rows of keyhole and horseshoes arches provide ventilation on each level, and large chatri and onion domes adorn the roof. In 2014 *Architectural Digest* included it in its list of the 26 most beautiful train stations in the world.
(Jln Sultan Hishamuddin; 🚇Kuala Lumpur)

## KTM Headquarters Building

HISTORIC BUILDING

3  Map p106, D4

Reportedly the last of the Mughal (or Indo-Saracenic) buildings in Kuala Lumpur, this handsome structure sits across from the Old KL Train Station. Grey where the train station is white, the building nonetheless mirrors much of the Mughal architecture, with rows of keyhole and horseshoe arches, onion domes and domed towers, and slim minarets. The building was completed in 1917 and is still in use.
(Jln Sultan Hishamuddin; 🚇Kuala Lumpur)

HELLIER/ALAMY ©

Old KL Train Station

## Brickfields Heritage Walk
WALKING TOUR

This 2½-hour guided walk, sponsored by KL City Hall, is held every Saturday at 8.30am. It's not necessary to book in advance, though it is recommended. The meeting place is the Vivekananda Ashram (see 6 ⊙ Map p106, C8). (☏2617 6273; www.visitkl.gov.my)

## Hundred Quarters
HISTORIC BUILDINGS

4 ⊙ Map p106, B7

These wonderfully photogenic housing rows, known as the Hundred Quarters, were built in 1920 to house railway employees and other civil servants. The multi-ethnic road names, Jln Rozario and Jln Chan Ah Tong, refer to two former chief clerks of the colonial civil service. Sadly, the ongoing redevelopment of Brickfields has put these heritage buildings under threat; residents have been given notice to vacate, but likely the buildings will still be standing when you visit. (Jln Rozario & Jln Chan Ah Tong; ☒KL Sentral)

## KL Butterfly Park
WILDLIFE RESERVE

5 ⊙ Map p106, C2

Billed as the largest enclosed butterfly garden in the world, this is a great place to get up close with a hundred or so of the 1100-plus butterfly species found in Malaysia, including the enormous and well-named birdwings, the elegant swallowtails, and the colourful tigers and jezebels. There's also a bug gallery where you can shudder at the size of Malaysia's giant centipedes and spiders. (Taman Rama Rama; ☏ 2693 4799; www.klbutterflypark.com; Jln Cenderasari; adult/child RM20/10; ⊙ 9am-6pm; ☒ Kuala Lumpur)

## Vivekananda Ashram
HERITAGE BUILDING

6 ◉ Map p106, B7

This ashram, built in 1904 and part of the global Ramakrishna movement, is a well-loved subject for photographers. It offers yoga courses, plus various social programs for the underprivileged. In 2014 the board of trustees sold the land with promises the old building would be preserved, though artist sketches show at best the ashram will be nestled under a commercial high-rise. (220 Jln Tun Sambanthan, Brickfields; ☒ KL Sentral)

**Local Life**

### Buddhist Maha Vihara

The **Buddhist Maha Vihara** (Map p106, C7; ☏ 2274 1141; www.buddhistmahavihara.com; 123 Jln Berhala; ☒ KL Sentral), founded in 1894 by Sinhalese settlers, is one of KL's major Theravada Buddhist temples. The temple is a particular hive of activity around **Wesak Day**, the Buddha's birthday, when a massive parade starts from here. Meditation classes (by donation) take place on Monday and Thursday at 8pm, chanting classes on Tuesday and Friday at 7.30pm.

## Sri Kandaswamy Temple
HINDU TEMPLE

7 ◉ Map p106, E6

This temple, fronted by an elaborate modern *gopuram* (gateway) was founded by the Sri Lankan community in 1909 as a place to practise Shaiva Siddhanta, a major Hindu sect popular with the diaspora community. One of the temple's major events (it has many festivals) is the 10-day **Mahotchava Festival** held around May or June, with celebrations including processions of the painted wooden deities. Check the temple's Facebook page for detailed information and schedules. (www.srikandaswamykovil.org; 3 Lg Scott; ⊙ 5.30am-9pm; monorail Tun Sambanthan)

## Masjid Negara
MOSQUE

8 ◉ Map p106, D3

The main place of worship for KL's Malay Muslim population is this gigantic mosque, inspired by Mecca's Grand Mosque. Able to accommodate 15,000 worshippers, its umbrella-like blue-tile roof has 18 points symbolising the 13 states of Malaysia and the five pillars of Islam. Rising above the mosque, a 74m-high minaret issues the call to prayer, which can be heard across Chinatown. Non-Muslims are welcome to visit outside prayer times; robes are available for those who are not dressed appropriately. (National Mosque; www.masjidnegara.gov.my/v2/; Jln Lembah Perdana; admission free; ⊙ 9am-noon, 3-4pm & 5.30-6.30pm, closed Fri morning; ☒ Kuala Lumpur)

## Understand
### We Built this City...with Bricks

In 1881, Kuala Lumpur, a town of wood and attap houses, burned to the ground. In the aftermath, brick became the material of choice for construction, a choice still evident in the look of KL's old neighbourhoods, and the name of one of its district.

Brickfields, as it is now called, was an area of abundant clay, and sat along the trade road into KL from the south; by the late 1880s nearly all of the kilns established to rebuild the city had been placed there. Later the KTM railway depot was constructed (now occupied by KL Sentral), and a large number of Sri Lankan and Indian Tamils brought in as railway employees and servants. Tamils have remarkably diverse religious backgrounds and today one finds in Brickfields Hindu and Buddhist temples, as well as Christian churches of various denominations.

In 2010 Brickfields was officially designated KL's 'Little India', what many considered a political move to win over voters. The neighbourhood is fast developing, but the streets from Jln Behara (Behara means 'shrine') northwest to Jln Tun Sambanthan, and Jln Scott, are still loaded with living heritage.

### Sree Veera Hanuman Temple    HINDU TEMPLE

9  Map p106, D5

Honouring Hanuman, this temple has been under reconstruction for years, and should be a striking sight when its *gopuram* is revealed: the tower rises with the coiled tail of the monkey god. Various puja (special prayer) services happen here – check the website for details.
(www.veerahanuman.com; Jln Scott; ☻7am-9pm; monorail Tun Sambanthan)

### Sam Kow Tong Temple    CHINESE TEMPLE

10  Map p106, C6

Established in 1916 by the Heng Hua clan, the 'three teachings' temple has a beautiful Hokkien-style temple roof, with graceful curving ridgelines that taper at the ends like swallowtails. The colourful rooftop dragons, and other figures, are actually three-dimensional mosaics, another traditional decorative feature of southern Chinese temples (though these are new works). Inside look for photos of the original temple, a simple timber-frame structure with a thatched roof.
(16 Jln Thambapillai; ☻7am-5pm; ☒KL Sentral)

## Majestic Spa SPA

11  Map p106, D4

Charles Rennie Macintosh's Willow Tea Rooms in Glasgow are the inspiration for the Majestic's delightful spa, where treatments are preceded by a refreshing tea or Pimms cocktail. After your pampering, there's a pool for a dip and sunbathe. A 90-minute massage starts at RM350.
(☏2785 8000; ww.majestickl.com; Majestic Hotel, 5 Jln Sultan Hishamuddin; ☒Kuala Lumpur)

# Eating

## Annalakshmi Vegetarian Restaurant INDIAN $

Long regarded as one of KL's best Indian vegetarian places, inside the fancy main hall at the Temple of Fine Arts (see 21 ☆ Map p106, C8), Annalakshmi has set prices at night and a daily lunch buffet for RM16; or you can choose to eat at the humbler Annalakshmi Riverside next to the car park behind the main building, where it's 'eat as you wish, give as you feel'.
(☏2272 3799; www.facebook.com/AnnalakshmiVegetarianRestaurantKualaLumpur; Temple of Fine Arts, 116 Jln Berhala; ☺11.30am-3pm & 6.30-10pm Tue-Sun; ☒; ☒KL Sentral)

## Vishal INDIAN $

12  Map p106, D5

Punters sit at two long rows of tables for the great banana-leaf meals served up at this long-running Brickfields favourite. Good for tiffin snacks and a refreshing lassi, too. If this place is busy it's a very similar deal at Vishalatchi, further along the road and run by the same family.
(☏2274 0502; 15 Jln Scott; meals RM5; ☺7am-10.30pm; ☒; monorail Tun Sambanthan)

## Kompleks Makan Tanglin HAWKER $

13  Map p106, D3

This small hawker complex up the hill behind Masjid Negara is a popular lunch spot for nearby workers and local families visiting the Lake Gardens. Try the *nasi lemak* (rice boiled in coconut milk, served with fried anchovies and peanuts), Hokkien mee or *ikan bakar* (grilled fish).
(Jln Cendarasari; meals RM5-10; ☺7am-4pm Mon-Sat; ☒Kuala Lumpur)

Top Tip

**Between the Gardens & Merdeka Square**

The entrance to the Tun Abdul Razak Heritage Park near the Islamic Arts Museum is about 1km from Merdeka Square. You can easily walk between these two areas along Jln Raja Laut. Another option is to rent a bicycle at KL by Cycle (p69) at Merdeka Square.

*Ikan bakar* (grilled fish)

## Jassal Tandoori Restaurant

INDIAN $$

14 ✗ Map p106, C6

One of Brickfields' best sit-down Indian restaurants, Jassal serves outstanding tandoori specialties, what must be the city's best dhal *makhani* (thick dark spicy lentils), and a load of other tasty dishes including a variety of naans, rotis and *parathas*. Cheap Indian beer is also on offer. (✆2274 6801; www.jesalsweethouse.com; 84 Jln Tun Sambanthan; dishes RM12-23; ⏰11am-11pm; 🚇KL Sentral)

## Hornbill Restaurant

MALAYSIAN $$

15 ✗ Map p106, C3

Providing a ringside view of the feathered inhabitants of KL Bird Park, this rustic place offers good food without gouging the tourists too much. Go local with its *nasi lemak* and fried noodles, or please the kids with fish and chips or the homemade chicken or beef burgers. (✆2693 8086; www.klbirdpark.com; KL Bird Park, 920 Jln Cenderawashi; mains RM13-27; ⏰9am-8pm; 📶; 🚇Kuala Lumpur)

## Understand

### A Primer on Islam

Though religious freedom is guaranteed under the constitution of Malaysia, the state religion is Islam and this affects everything in Kuala Lumpur from traffic patterns (especially with Friday afternoon prayers), to media freedom, to the price of alcohol.

Most Malaysian Muslims are Sunnis, but all Muslims share a common belief in the Five Pillars of Islam:

**Shahadah** (the declaration of faith) 'There is no God but Allah; Mohammed is his Prophet.'

**Salat** (prayer) – Ideally five times a day, in which the muezzin (prayer leader) calls the faithful to prayer from the minarets of every mosque. You will hear these hauntingly beautiful calls throughout the day.

**Zakat** (almsgiving) – Donating 2.5% of one's wealth to the poor.

**Sawm** (fasting) – Includes observing the fasting month of Ramadan. This is actually a wonderful time to visit the city as Ramadan markets are set up everywhere, and a festive rather than solemn spirit prevails.

**Hajj** (pilgrimage to Mecca) – Every Muslim aspires to do the hajj at least once and there are special banks set up for saving, such as the Tabung Haji (p49).

Muslim dietary laws forbid alcohol, pork and all pork-based products. Restaurants where it's OK for Muslims to dine will be clearly labelled 'halal'.

A radical Islamic movement has not taken firm root in Malaysia but religious conservatism has grown over recent years: many feel it has gotten worse since the ruling party UMNO lost its supermajority in 2008, and subsequently the popular vote in 2013.

For foreign visitors, the most obvious sign is the national obsession with propriety, and on perceived insults to Islam. Reading the local papers reveals cases of Bibles being confiscated, warnings against encouraging dog-friendly events, and attempts to give sharia courts the same powers as federal courts. Probably the most obvious change in recent years is that more Muslim women wear the hijab (a head covering also known regionally as the *tudong*).

## Fierce Curry House INDIAN $$

**16**  Map p106, A7

There's outdoor and indoor seating at this biryani specialty restaurant just west of Little India in Bangsar. Choose from mutton, chicken, or even lobster (order the day before) biryanis, veggie thali sets (RM8) and banana-leaf meals on the weekend. This place hams itself up online but is actually very low-key. (2202 3456; www.facebook.com/FierceCurryHouse; 16 Jln Kemuja; biryani RM15-18; 7.30am-10.30pm; Bangsar)

## Colonial Cafe MALAYSIAN, INTERNATIONAL $$$

**17**  Map p106, D4

British Malay cuisine, as interpreted by Hainanese chefs of yore, is on the menu at this elegant restaurant in the heritage wing of the Majestic, probably the best spot in KL to feel the privilege and grace of the colonial era. Highlights of the menu include the Caesar salad, chicken rice served Melaka style, and the Hainanese chicken chop. (2785 8000; www.majestickl.com; Majestic Hotel, 5 Jln Sultan Hishamuddin; mains RM75-210; 11.30am-2.30pm & 6.30-11pm; ; Kuala Lumpur)

### Local Life
## Little India's Street Food

Brickfields is loaded with good choices for street food. For cheap eats such as *roti canai* or banana-leaf meals try the **Little India Fountain Hawker Stalls** (Map p106, B7; dishes RM5-10; 24hr; KL Sentral) across from the gaudy central fountain. **Brickfields Pisang Goreng** (Map p106, C6; cnr Jln Thambapillai & Jln Tun Sambanthan 4; fritters RM1.20; 10am-6pm; monorail Tun Sambanthan) has delicious fried bananas, while across the street outside the 7-Eleven store, **ABC Stall** (Map p106, C6; Jln Tun Sambanthan 4; cendol RM1.90; 10am-10pm; monorail Tun Sambanthan) serves fresh coconut juice, *ais cendol* (shaved ice) and other desserts.

# Drinking

## MAI Bar COCKTAIL BAR

**18**  Map p106, C6

This Polynesian tiki bar, which goes a little too heavy on the red lights, is another addition to KL's growing (and often glowing) band of high-rise bars with panoramic city views. DJs spin Wednesday to Saturday after 10pm. For a more casual atmosphere, and live music Friday nights, try the hotel's W XYZ bar. (www.aloftkualalumpursentral.com; Aloft Kuala Lumpur Sentral, 5 Jln Stesen Sentral; noon-midnight, to 2am Fri & Sat; ; KL Sentral)

TK KURIKAWA/SHUTTERSTOCK ©

Nu Sentral

### Tea Lounge TEAHOUSE

19  Map p106, D4

Enjoy classic British high tea, and impeccable service, in the lounge of this lovely colonial-era hotel. If you wish to drink in the Orchid Conservatory make a reservation. (☏2785 8000; www.majestickl.com; Majestic Hotel, 5 Jln Sultan Hishamuddin; ☺3-6pm; ☒Kuala Lumpur)

### Drawing Room TEAHOUSE

20  Map p106, A3

Enjoy proper British high tea in the original drawing room or verandah of the Carcosa Seri Negara hotel, in the hills just northwestern of Lake Perdana. This heritage mansion was built at the turn of the 20th century by Sir Frank Swettenham, the man who gave impetus for the creation of the lake and the Lake Gardens. (☏2295 0888; reservation@carcosa.com.my; Carcosa Seri Negara; ☺3pm-6pm)

# Entertainment

### Temple of Fine Arts THEATRE

21  Map p106, C8

Classical Indian dance and music shows take place here throughout the year. The centre also runs performing-arts courses. See the website for schedules. (☏2274 3709; www.tfa.org.my; 116 Jln Berhala; ☺closed Mon; ☒KL Sentral, monorail KL Sentral)

# Shopping

### Lavanya Arts
ARTS, CRAFTS

Lavanya, inside the Temple of Fine Arts (see 21 ⭐ Map p106, C8), sells colourful craft goods including adorable kids' and adults' clothes, and home decorations. Come the week around Deepavali for a festive range of beautiful Indian tribal arts, as well as handsome painted wooden dolls, brass sculpture, and colourful furniture from Rajastan. (www.facebook.com/lavanyaarts; Temple of Fine Arts, 114-116 Jln Berhala; ☺10am-9.30pm Tue-Sat, to 3pm Sun; 🚇KL Sentral)

### Sonali
FASHION

22 🔒 Map p106, E6

Sequins, silks, filigree patterns and tie-dye – all the elements of the flash Bollywood look are present in this boutique. It's mainly for women but also has some fancy tops for men. (www.sonali.com.my; 67A Jln Scott; ☺10am-7pm Mon-Sat; 🚇Tun Sanbanthan)

### Wei-Ling Gallery
ART

23 🔒 Map p106, D5

The top two floors of this old shophouse have been turned into a gallery to showcase local artists. Note the artwork covering the metal security gate in front of the shophouse next door.

## Top Tip

### Lightning Strikes

Malaysia has the world's second-highest incidence of lightning strikes, and deaths are sadly very frequent. Storms appear suddenly over KL, especially during autumn. It's important to keep an eye on the weather forecast and to restrict outdoor activities such as visiting the Lake Gardens to the morning when there is less likelihood of a storm. If you are caught in a storm seek shelter, preferably in a large building (not just a gazebo), and keep away from electrical devices (especially any plugged in).

(www.weiling-gallery.com; 8 Jln Scott; ☺10am-6pm Mon-Fri, 10am-5pm Sat, Sun by appointment only; 🚇KL Sentral)

### Nu Sentral
MALL

24 🔒 Map p106, C6

The city's newest mall is part of the ongoing development of KL Sentral. Here you'll find (if you can find anything in this labyrinth complex) a branch of Parkson department store, MPH bookstore, a GSC multiplex and a food court. (www.nusentral.com; 1 Sentral Jln Travers; ☺10am-10pm; 🚇KL Sentral)

Top Sights
# Thean Hou Temple

### Getting There

Monorail Tun Samban-than then taxi.

**Taxi** From downtown.

Sitting atop leafy Robson Heights, this imposing multistorey Chinese temple, dedicated to Thean Hou, the heavenly queen, affords wonderful views over Kuala Lumpur. Opened in 1989 by the Selangor and Federal Territory Hainan Association, it serves as both a house of worship and a functional space for events such as weddings. In recent years it's also become a tourist attraction in its own right, especially during Chinese festival times and the birthdays of the various temple gods.

# Don't Miss

### Architecture & Arts

The temple is a hodgepodge of Chinese regional and historical styles, and is impressive more for its size and atmosphere than craftsmanship (the entire complex is mostly concrete and eyerollingly gaudy in places). Some of its most attractive features include the sweeping ridgeline of the main hall, which tapers out like a swallowtail – this is a traditional Hokkien design for important buildings. The dragons and phoenixes on the highest eaves are examples of a type of 3D hand-laid mosaic commonly used as decoration in southern Chinese temples. Examine them up close from the top level.

### Main Prayer Hall

Thean Hou takes centre stage in the main hall on the 3rd floor, with Kuan Yin (the bodhisattva of compassion) on her right and Shuiwei Shengniang (goddess of the waterfront) to her left. In front of Thean Hou's knees, look for her two guardians, known as Eyes-that-see-a-thousand-miles and Ears-that-hear-on-the-wind. Above Thean Hou note the inverted ceiling, a traditional design in her temples. If you wish to learn your fortune pick up the sticks near the altar, and drop them back in their jar so that one sticks up the tallest. The number on this one will correspond to a drawer containing a paper with your fortune on it.

### Views

From the temple's courtyard and pavilions you can look down across the city and see Menara KL and the Petronas Towers off in the distance. It's a good vantage point to watch the sunset.

RAJ AN MADHAVAN/GETTY IMAGES ©

---

☎ 2274 7088

www.hainannet.com.my/en

off Jln Syed Putra

🕐 8am-10pm

☑ **Top Tips**

▶ Combine a visit to the temple with the Royal Museum (p104), getting your taxi to pass through the rolling grounds of the historic Kwong Tong Cemetery on the way.

▶ The liveliest times at the temple are during Chinese New Year, Wesak Day (the Buddha's birthday) and the days around Thean Hou's birthday (23rd day of the third lunar month).

▶ If you take a taxi it's best to ask the driver to wait, as it can be hard to get a taxi back otherwise.

✕ **Take a Break**

There's a food court on the ground floor for *nasi lemak* and snacks, or head to nearby Little India for excellent hawker food (p115).

# Local Life
# Boutique-Hopping in Bangsar Baru

This former rubber plantation district turned wealthy suburb is where new trends in shopping and eating come to live (and then die before they lose their edge). In a few compact blocks you'll find terraced restaurants and specialty cafes, artisanal bakeries luring passers-by with the aroma of fresh bread and homemade sandwiches, plus Indian nail art salons, aspiring local designers and two high-end malls.

## Getting There

Bangsar Baru is east of Brickfields.

🚕 **Taxi** A taxi from downtown is easiest.

🚈 **LRT** Bangsar then taxi.

**❶ Silverfish Books**

Pick up a tome at this local bookshop and **publisher** (📞2284 4837; www.silverfishbooks.com; 28-1 Jln Telawi; ⏱10am-8pm Mon-Fri, to 6pm Sat & Sun) of contemporary Malaysian literature. It often hosts talks – we once saw Nobel laureate Joseph Stiglitz here.

**❷ Brunch at G3 Kitchen & Bar**

Bangsar is loaded with an impressive range of eating options. A good stop for brunch is **G3 Kitchen & Bar** (19 Jln Telawi 3; mains RM22-33; ⏱11am-11pm Mon-Fri, 9am-11pm Sat & Sun; 🛜). Sit in the cosy indoor space or outside on the terrace and devour wood-fired "pizzas, made-from-scratch burgers and sandwiches, and fresh juices.

**❸ Never Follow Suit**

This vintage and original design **boutique** (📞2284 7316; 28-2, Jln Telawi 2; ⏱11am-9pm Tue-Sun) is a good first stop for the fashion-conscious. Also look for **Shoes Shoes Shoes** (www.facebook.com/ShoesShoesShoes3; 2nd fl, Jln Telawi 3; ⏱11am-9pm), the dream project of shoe fanatic **Nurita Harith** (www.nuritaharith.com; 2nd fl, Jln Telawi 3, beside Alexis Bistro; ⏱10am-6pm Tue-Sun), one of KL's hot young designers.

**❹ Devi's Corner**

If you need a snack, nearly every street intersection seems to have a venerable Indian joint. At **Devi's Corner** (14 Jln Telawi 2; dishes RM1.5-7.5; ⏱24hr) the thali sets are excellent, and you can also get thosa (crispy pancakes), biryani, tan-

doori chicken and great satay. Another solid choice is nearby banana-leaf meal seller **Sri Nirwana Maju** (📞2287 8445; 43 Jln Telawi 3; meals RM10-20; ⏱10am-1.30pm).

**❺ Bangsar Village I & II**

These twin **malls** (www.bangsarvillage.com; cnr Jln Telawi 1 & Jln Telawi 2; ⏱10am-10pm) are linked by a covered bridge and house upmarket crafts and fashions. Try **Dude & the Duchess** for fashion, **Thomas Chan** for shoes, and **Desiree** for clothes with a touch of Chinese styling. Bangsar Village II also has a **play centre** (www.kizsports.com.my; admission RM28) for kids.

**❻ Relax at Hammam Spa**

This mosaic-tiled Moroccan **spa** (📞2282 2180; www.hammamspas.com; 3rd fl, Bangsar Village II; ⏱10am-10.30pm) is located in Bangsar Village II. Couples and singles packages are available with titles such as the Royal Couple (RM688) and the Sultan's Daughter Wedding (RM428). A simple *gommage* (steam and scrub) will set you back RM150.

**❼ A Beer at the Social**

The **Social** (www.thesocial.com.my; 57-59 Jln Telawi 3; ⏱11.30am-2am) has pool tables, good food and cheap happy-hour draught to quaff on its long terrace. **Ril's Bangsar** (📞2201 3846; www.facebook.com/RilsBangsar; 30 Jln Telawi 5; ⏱10am-2am; 🛜), a premium-grade steak restaurant on street level, has a prohibition-era style cocktail bar upstairs. There's live music (jazz, blues, soul) on weekends.

# The Best of
# Kuala Lumpur

**Kuala Lumpur's Best Walks**

A Stroll Through Kampung Baru ... 124

Chinatown Architecture Ramble .. 126

**Kuala Lumpur's Best...**

Street Food & Food Courts ........ 128

Bars & Cafes .................... 130

Shopping ...................... 132

With Kids...................... 134

For Free ...................... 135

Clubs & Entertainment .......... 136

Religious & Heritage Buildings ..... 138

Green Spaces .................. 139

Museums & Galleries............. 140

Spas & Wellness ................ 142

T-shirts for sale, Central Market (p78)
LAURIE NOBLE/GETTY IMAGES ©

# Best Walks
# A Stroll Through Kampung Baru

## 🏃 The Walk

Beyond the city's blockbuster sights, this walk offers a fascinating tour of the village side of KL, passing traditional wood houses on stilts, the religious buildings and shrines of multiple faiths, and great places to snack on local dishes. There's not much shade on this walk so start early or head out after 4pm. Dress conservatively (a scarf to cover the head is recommended for women) as you will be entering a mosque and Sikh temple.

**Start** Chow Kit monorail station

**Finish** Dang Wangi LRT station

**Length** 3.5km; two hours

## ✕ Take a Break

If you need refreshment at the start of the walk there are stalls inside Bazaar Baru Chow Kit (p88). Otherwise, halfway through the tour, there is a row of Malay restaurants along Jln Raja Muda Musa.

Street stalls, Kampung Baru

### ❶ Wood House & Shrine

Walk south on Jln TAR, and turn right into Jln Chow Kit to No 41, a tiny wooden house squashed between buildings. On the way back check out the **shrine** across the parking lot. This is a Datuk Gong, where Chinese worship ancient Malay spirits alongside their own earth god.

### ❷ Bazaar Baru Chow Kit

Return to Jln TAR and cross over to lively **Bazaar Baru Chow Kit** (p88). At the back of the market, just past the turn for Lrg Raja Bot, check out the pretty Chinese temple and row of painted wood houses.

### ❸ Tatt Khalsa Diwan Gurdwara

Just down Lrg Raja Bot you'll see this **Sikh temple** (p86), the largest in Southeast Asia.

### ❹ Masjid Jamek Kampung Baru

Further along Jln Raja Alang is the area's beautiful **mosque** (p86).

### 5 Viewpoint

Where Jln Raja Alang turns south, continue on the smaller road to a two-level apartment block: two palms in a small field here perfectly frame the Petronas Towers.

### 6 Rumah Limas

At the junction of Jln Raja Muda Musa and Jln Raja Mahadi stands the turquoise-and-white **Rumah Limas**, built in 1913; explore Jln Raja Mahadi and the cross streets for more traditional wooden houses.

### 7 Sultan Sulaiman Club

Cross Jln Raja Abdullah and then turn left on Jln Datuk Abdul Razak. Continue to the handsome black-and-white painted **Sultan Sulaiman Club** (p86), accessible through a gate.

### 8 Master Mat's House

Just past the club down a side street to the right is **Master Mat's House**. Built in 1921 by a beloved English-school headmaster, this charming blue house sits on

stone pillars and sports a curved white staircase.

### 9 Jalan Khatib Koyan

Heading south down Jln Raja Abdullah, take **Jln Khatib Koyan**, Kampung Baru's most charming back street. It ends with a great **food court** back at the intersection with Jln Raja Abdullah.

### 10 Dang Wangi Houses

At the turn to Dang Wangi LRT station there is a last cluster of **wood houses**.

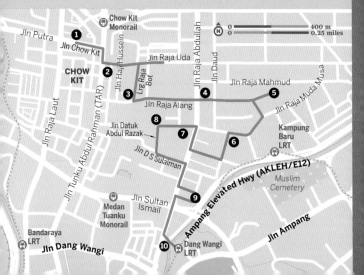

# Best Walks
# Chinatown Architecture Ramble

## 🏃 The Walk

The focus of this walk is the variety of architecture found in the oldest part of town: from eclectic two- and three-storey shophouses to Cantonese-style temples, Dravidian-style Hindu temples, art deco buildings and a Mughal-style mosque. There are endless places to snack, and as most of the walk is covered you can do this any time of day in comfort.

**Start** Maharajalela monorail station

**Finish** Masjid Jamek LRT station

**Length** 2km; two hours

## 🍴 Take a Break

Stop at Peter Hoe Beyond Cafe (p73) for coffee and a light meal, or Petaling Street Market (p79) for a coconut or sugar-cane juice pick-me-up.

Petaling Street Market (p79), Chinatown

### ❶ Chan She Shu Yuen Clan Temple

From Maharajalela monorail station head north to the busy traffic roundabout of Bulatan Merdeka, and look for this ornate **clan temple** (p66). Spend a little time studying the lively Shek Wan pottery.

### ❷ Sri Mahamariamman Temple

Then head up to the **Petaling Street Market** (p79) entrance: pop in if it looks enticing, otherwise head to Jln Tun HS Lee. The shophouses here are among Chinatown's oldest; further up note the sunken arcade walkways. Take a break inside the **Sri Mahamariamman Temple** (p66).

### ❸ Guandi Temple

Cross the road to visit this **temple** (p68) of the patron of righteous brotherhoods. You could also pop into the covered market to the right.

### ❹ Lee Rubber Building

Cross back over Jln Tun HS Lee for the pale-yellow art deco **Lee**

**Rubber Building** built in 1930. You can explore the inside via the 1st-floor bookstore, or Peter Hoe Beyond on the 2nd floor.

### ❺ Sin Sze Si Ya Temple

Cross Jln Tun Tan Cheng Lock and turn left to the atmospheric **Sin Sze Si Ya Temple** (p66), built by Hakka and KL founder Yap Ah Loy.

### ❻ Central Market

Exit the back of the temple and turn left on Lebuh Pudu to reach **Central Market** (p67), one of KL's most hand-some art deco buildings. Adjacent is an equally handsome row of restored shophouses with eclectic European facades.

### ❼ Medan Pasar

Continue up to this **square** (p69), once the home of Kapitan Yap Ah Loy, backed by rows of restored three-storey shophouses in a range of early 20th-century styles; note the Dutch gables on the front left shops and the lovely art deco clock tower from the 1930s in the centre.

### ❽ Lebuh Ampang

Continue up **Lebuh Ampang** (p68) to Jln Gereja. The shophouses near the end belong to Indian merchants and moneylenders called Chettiars.

### ❾ Masjid Jamek

Retrace your steps to Jln Tun Perak to visit this Mughal-inspired **mosque** (p66) and to see the revitalisation of the heritage riverfront area (the River of Life project).

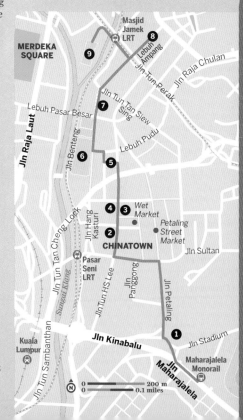

# Best
# Street Food & Food Courts

PAUL KENNEDY/GETTY IMAGES ©

KL's tastiest and best-value food is found at hawker stalls, and locals are fiercely loyal to their favourite vendors. Many hawkers have been in business for decades, and the best enjoy reputations that exceed their geographical reach. In KL the definition of street food is broad, taking in dishes served at individual stalls on wheels, at food courts, and in traditional *kopitiam* (coffee shops).

### The Hawker Scene

Hawker stalls can be found individually roadside, or more often in clusters at a food court, or under a giant spreading tree at the edge of a parking lot. Food courts sometimes have a mix of Indian, Malay and Chinese dishes, but often one ethnic cuisine will be featured. Don't miss the *mamak* food courts, serving snack foods, such as tandoori chicken and murtabak from KL's Muslim Indian-Malay community.

*Kopitiam*, whether owned by an individual or run like a food court with multiple outlets under a single roof, are also considered part of the scene and are as inexpensive as the outdoor venues.

If you need air-con, head to KL's equally renowned mall food courts, which often have outlets of the same hawker venues found outside.

### Ordering

At a multiple vendor joint, place an order with whoever you like, find a seat and pay for each dish as it's delivered to your table. At food courts, *kopitiam* and *mamak* joints someone will usually approach you to take your order. You'll also usually be approached by someone taking drink orders after you've sat down – pay for these separately as well. Note that beer is not generally available.

☑ **Top Tip**

▶ If you're intrigued by the food you've sampled in KL and feel you want a bit of expert guidance to help you learn and sample more, consider a food tour with **Simply Enak** (☏017-287 8929; www. simplyenak.com; tours RM200-250). At the time of press its tours included Chinatown and Chow Kit with prices including food and drinks, as well as a few cultural highlights.

Jalan Alor (p25)

## Best Hawker Food

**Little India Fountain Hawker Stalls** Two-storey collection of stalls for roti or banana-leaf meals. (p115)

**Keong Kee** Sit under a tree with a coconut curry or wild-boar curry. (p39)

**Jalan Alor** KL's most famous food street, with dozens of choices. (p25)

**Kin Kin** Universally loved originator of chilli *pan mee*. (p88)

## Best Food Courts

**Lot 10 Hutong** Enjoy famous hawker food in an air-conditioned food court. (p25)

**Dharma Realm Guan Yin Sagely Monastery Canteen** Best veggie buffet in town. (p51)

**Restoran Win Heng Seng** Popular local breakfast food court. (p25)

## Best Food Markets

**Imbi Market** Traditional breakfast (including *kopi*) in an outdoor stall area of a wet market. (p24)

**Madras Lane Hawkers** Chinatown back alley lined with stalls serving *yong tau fu* and *bak kut teh*. (p72)

## Best Kopitiam

**Yut Kee** Serving Hainanese comfort dishes such as chicken chops since 1928. (p90)

**Capital Café** Beloved multi-hawker venue for Malay and Chinese dishes. (p89)

**Hong Ngek** This long-running Chinatown joint serves excellent ginger duck and ribs in Guinness. (p69)

## Best Mamak Food Courts

**Restoran Yusoof dan Zakhir** Southern Indian food in a cool green-and-yellow shophouse. (p71)

**Nasi Kandar Pelita** Choose from 60 succulent dishes at this bungalow on stilts. (p50)

# Best
# **Bars & Cafes**

Despite Malaysia's Muslim majority, KL has a lively and varied drinking scene that includes sophisticated lounges and speakeasy bars, British-style pubs, Spanish tapas bars, and several streets cheek-to-jowl with alcohol-fuelled options. During the day the selections for whetting your whistle are no less varied, with traditional tea and *kopi* available in ageing shophouses, and lattes and single-origin coffee in a range of hip cafes.

JON ARNOLD/GETTY IMAGES ©

☑ **Top Tip**

▶ Upscale bars (and clubs) usually have a dress code.

▶ Keep up to date on KL's latest bars with **TimeOut Kuala Lumpur** (www.timeout.com/kuala-lumpur).

## Sky Bars

Sky-high taxes make a night out boozing an expensive affair, but KL sort of makes up for that by offering such fabulous city views from its many elevated venues. You can't drink in the iconic Petronas Towers themselves, but the view is better gazing *at* them from another rooftop bar.

## Bars

The speakeasy scene is well matured in KL, though ironically many venues sit inside shopping malls, which somewhat spoils the effect. Regular bars are concentrated in the Golden Triangle (especially Changkat Bukit Bintang), Bangsar and Pavilion KL shopping mall. For gay nightlife options see p55.

## Cafes

KL has had a coffee scene for over a hundred years, and traditional *kopitiam* (coffee shops) still serve a potent brew. *Kopi* can be an acquired taste, but there are also tea drinks (and a beverage called *cham*, which is a mix of tea and coffee). Modern cafes are also popular, both chains and individual shops, and there is a growing specialty coffee scene worth checking out.

## Best Bars for Casual Drinking

**Pisco Bar** This hip tapas bar is set back from the street in a revamped shophouse. (p31)

**Taps Beer Bar** KL's best selection of craft beers from around the world. (p31)

**Reggae Bar** Relaxed Chinatown bar. (p74)

**Green Man** This British-style pub on KL's premier bar street has a loyal following. (p34)

Heli Lounge Bar (p54)

## Best Sky Bars & Lounges

**Frangipani** There's a deck bar streetside and a fashionable gay-friendly lounge upstairs. (p31)

**Fuego** Enjoy innovative cocktails in a sky-high perch with exceptional views of the Twin Towers. (p53)

**Heli Lounge Bar** Mind the lack of a railing as you drink in the views across to Menara KL from this rooftop bar. (p54)

**Sky Bar** This high-end lounge in the Trader's Hotel offers stunning city views. (p54)

## Best Cafes & Teahouses

**Tea Lounge** Enjoy British high tea in the colonial-era Majestic Hotel. (p116)

**VCR** Single-origin espresso and hand-drip coffees in a spacious remodelled shophouse. (p39)

**Feeka Coffee Roasters** Enjoy both good food and coffee at this Jln Mesui hang out with indoor and outdoor seating. (p29)

**Yut Kee** Try traditional *kopi* in this Hainanese *kopitiam* running since 1928. (p90)

## Worth a Trip

Upstairs from the restaurant of the same name, **Hit & Mrs** (☎ 2282 3571; 15 Lg Kurau; ⊙ 5pm-1am Tue-Sat; 🗦; 🚇 Bangsar) is a casual cocktail bar on a quiet strip outside the main commercial area of Bangsar. The design is retro cool, with rattan chairs and frosted glass, and encourages a long stay.

# Best
# Shopping

Shopping in KL is dominated by mega-malls with similar selections of international brands, but the homeland of Jimmy Choo also supports plenty of local designers, a decent legacy of traditional crafts and vintage goods, and a number of bustling markets from which you're at least going to return home with loads of interesting photos.

LAURIE NOBLE/GETTY IMAGES ©

## Traditional Arts & Crafts

Skilled artisans are a dying breed but a few crafts are still going strong in KL, such as pewterware, batik and basketry. It's also not hard to find good-quality antique and vintage items in independently owned shops (such as in Central Market), and newer works in museum gift shops. The city's frequent arts festivals are also good places to pick up local crafts. Browsing the incense and statuary shops around Chinese temples, and the flower stalls around Hindu temples, is also interesting. Markets, on the other hand, such as Petaling Street (p79) and Masjid India's *pasar malam* (night market), are hit-and-miss, selling mostly cheap clothing and counterfeit modern goods.

## Local Designers

Look for traditional *kebaya* and shoemakers, high-end and hipster fashion designers, as well as chains such as British India that sell well-made clothing suitable for a tropical climate. None of this is a bargain, though; expect to pay what you would in an independent boutique in a European city.

## Best Malls

**Pavilion KL** The gold standard for KL's mall scene. (p36)

**Suria KLCC** A retail nirvana at the base of the Petronas Towers. (p59)

**Fahrenheit88** Youth-oriented mall, great for Japanese fashions. (p36)

## Best Boutiques

**British India** Popular home-grown chain selling well-made linen clothing for the tropics. (p36)

**Never Follow Suit** Quirky-cool boutique run by young designers. (p121)

**Ang Eng** For traditional *kebaya* (blouses; p58)

**Aseana** A multibrand boutique showcasing the works of many local design stars. (p59)

Central Market (p78)

## Best Arts & Crafts

**Kompleks Kraf** Large government-run craft shop for kites, baskets, pewter, ceramics and more. (p58)

**Peter Hoe Beyond** Tons of colourful custom-made fabrics and unique household items. (p78)

**Central Market** Dozens of shops selling local arts and crafts under one roof. (p78)

**Royal Selangor** Traditional maker of lovely handcrafted pewter. (p36)

**Lavanya Arts** Authentic Indian arts and crafts. (p117)

**Museum of Ethnic Arts** Stunning ethnic crafts from all over Malaysia such as wood carvings, masks, embroidery and paintings. (p68)

**Islamic Arts Museum** Good for art books and textiles. (p102)

### Worth a Trip

Just north of town is the famed **Royal Selangor Visitor Centre** (☏ 4145 6122; http://visitorcentre. royalselangor.com; 4 Jln Usahawan 6, Setepak Jaya; ⊙ 9am-5pm; ☒ Wangsa Maju, then taxi) of pewterware fame, where you can buy beautiful hand-crafted pieces or try your hand in the DIY workshop. Tin mining and pewter are near synonymous with KL history, so a gift from here is as unique as they come.

# Best
# With Kids

With its plethora of colourful, accessible and most importantly yummy street and food court eats and easy-to-sell attractions such as jungle canopy walks and tower lookouts, KL makes a good destination for families. Public transport is manageable, taxis are ubiquitous, parks are fairly plentiful, and accommodation is clean and modern.

### Eating Out

Hygiene at restaurants and hawker stalls is generally good. With choices that range from fish-head curry to Western comfort foods it's easy to please both adventurous and fickle young appetites. Dehydration is a concern in the heat so be sure to monitor kids' fluid intake.

### Best Attractions for Kids

**FRIM** Spot wild monkeys and brave a canopy walk. (p97)

**Batu Caves** The colourful tableaux of Hindu myths, wild monkeys, and the Dark Cave capture children's imagination. (p95)

**Bank Negara Malaysia Museum & Art Gallery** Walk through a tunnel lined with RM1 million. (p84)

**Aquaria KLCC** In the heart of KL, kids can interact with sea creatures. (p43)

**KL Bird Park** This massive free-flight aviary filled with exotic birds is a family highlight. (p101)

**Petronas Towers** View the city from on high and learn about the construction of the iconic buildings. (p42)

**Menara KL** Take a jungle walk before or after a ride up this telecommunications tower. (p44)

**Petrosains** A good hands-on kids science centre. (p49)

CHRISTIAN KOBER/ROBERT HARDING ©

### ☑ Top Tips

▶ **TimeOut KL** (www.timeout.com/kuala-lumpur/kids) publishes a *Malaysia for Kids* guide and has up-to-date listings and features on what to do with your kids on its website.

▶ Breastfeeding in public is frowned upon, and should be discreet if necessary. Carrying babies in a sling is easier than a pram due to the uneven sidewalks. Midrange and upscale restaurants often have highchairs but budget places don't.

▶ A slow-moving family, especially one with a pram, can be a target for theft. Always be vigilant.

# Best
# For Free

Much of the best of KL is completely free for visitors. This includes all temples and mosques, public parks, some museums, and many architecturally interesting buildings, such as Chinatown shophouses. People-watching along busy streets and in markets are also fun activities that don't break the bank. And there are free tours of Brickfields (p109), Merdeka Square (p67) and Kampung Baru (p84).

STUART DEE/GETTY IMAGES ©

## Best Free Sights & Activities

**Royal Malaysia Police Museum** Fascinating museum charting Malaysia's history of policing. (p101)

**KL City Gallery** Get an overview of KL's history and diverse architecture. (p63)

**Bank Negara Malaysia Museum & Art Gallery** Surprisingly interesting exhibits on money, including rare coins. (p84)

**KLCC Park** Beautiful trees and views of the Twin Towers. (p43)

**Chan She Shu Yuen Clan Association Temple** Admire the Cantonese design and fine pottery figures from China on the roof. (p66)

**Sri Mahamariamman Temple** This temple is always a buzzing hive of religious and festival activity. (p66)

**Sin Sze Si Ya Temple** KL's oldest Chinese temple has a deep devotional atmosphere. (p66)

**Masjid Jamek** A centre of worship and a beautiful building in the Indo-Saracenic style. (p66)

**National Textiles Museum** Displays the range of local textiles with beautiful examples. (p63)

**Merdeka Square** Malaysia's independence square is surrounded by handsome colonial architecture. (p62)

**KL Forest Eco Park** A real jungle right in the heart of the city. (p45)

**Badan Warisan Malaysia** This heritage society has preserved a stunning example of traditional stilt housing. (p48)

**Museum of Ethnic Arts** Splendid private collection of arts and crafts from Malaysia and abroad. (p68)

**Batu Caves** The main cave of this Hindu shrine is free; the psychedelic Ramayana Cave is only RM2. (p95)

**Perdana Botanical Garden** Explore exotic native and foreign plants then stroll the lovely Lake Perdana. (p101)

# Best Clubs & Entertainment

PETER CHAN/AGEPHOTO ©

KL has plenty of entertainment options, from live music and big-scale musicals to traditional arts performances. Aside from religious festivities and a couple of established art and film events, there aren't a lot of other festivals on the annual calendar, though many one-off events are highly worth attending. In general, there's a lot happening, but it's not always well advertised. The websites and Facebook links below are invaluable for keeping up to date.

## Clubs & Live Music

Wednesday to Sunday are the main club nights, with different events on to suit all tastes and budgets. Be prepared for cover charges, which vary greatly (usually around RM18 to RM60), but usually include one drink. Some clubs deny entry to under 21s. KL has a good live-music scene, and you can catch anything from a novice guitarist strumming in a shophouse cafe to accomplished jazz performers and international pop music artists. **TimeOut Kuala Lumpur** (www.timeout.com/kuala-lumpur/music-nightlife) keeps an updated list of upcoming gigs.

## Traditional & Modern Arts Performances

Traditional performances of shadow puppetry, opera, dance, drumming and drama, as well as modern arts festivals, are becoming more common. Keep up with events by checking the websites of NGOs and art groups such as Pusaka (p90), **Kakiseni** (www.facebook.com/mykakiseni), **Daily Seni** (www.facebook.com/DailySeni), and **MapKl** (www.facebook.com/mapkl). More commercial Broadway-style musicals and plays are also popular, though censorship demands mean they are rarely more than simple entertainment.

## Best Live Music

**KL Live** Large venue for rock and pop concerts. (p56)

**No Black Tie** Chic live-music bar run by a classical pianist. (p35)

**Dewan Filharmonik Petronas** Gorgeous concert hall at the base of the Petronas Towers. (p56)

**Alexis Ampang** Popular live jazz venue. (p93)

## Best Traditional & Modern Performances

**Kelantan Shadow Puppet Play** Traditional shadow puppet performances daily. (p76)

**Panggung Bandaraya** KL's most beautiful theatrical space is set in a fabulous old colonial building. (p76)

Istana Budaya (p91)

**Petaling Street Art House** A range of Chinese performance arts are held in this shophouse in Chinatown. (p77)

**Sutra Dance Theatre** Dance legend Ramli Ibrahim's performance studio near Lake Titiwangsa. (p91)

**Istana Budaya** The national theatre holds big-scale drama and musical performances. (p91)

**Temple of Fine Arts** For high-quality classical Indian dance and music performances. (p116)

## Best Clubs

**Zouk** Popular club with various spaces on different levels to suit different tastes and budgets. (p55)

**Frangipani** Sophisticated lounge and club on buzzing Changkat Bukit Bintang. (p31)

**Blueboy Discotheque** KL's oldest running gay club. (p34)

## Worth a Trip

Part of the Sentul West regeneration project, the **Kuala Lumpur Performing Arts Centre** (KLPAC; ✆4047 9000; www.klpac.org; Jln Strachan, Sentul Park; ®Sentul), set in an old railway warehouse, puts on a wide range of events including dramas, musicals, dance, film festivals (non-censored) and exhibitions. Also on offer are performing arts courses, and with any luck the **Yayasan Sime Darby Arts Festival** will become a yearly event here.

# Best
# Religious &
# Heritage Buildings

KL was first forged by the labours of Chinese, Indians and Malays, all very religiously oriented peoples who, not surprisingly, have left the city with a splendid legacy of temples and mosques. The fourth major party in the city's development, the British, bequeathed a colonial architectural heritage that runs from Tudor-style clubhouses to grand railway stations inspired by the Mughal empire in India.

DAVID HILL/GETTY IMAGES ©

## Best Temples & Mosques

**Masjid Jamek** This former national mosque was built in a handsome Mughal style in 1907. (p66)

**Chan She Shu Yuen Clan Association Temple** One of the few Chinese temples in KL with abundant decorative arts. (p66)

**Sin Sze Si Ya Temple** Founded by Kapitan Yap Ah Loy in 1864, this is still a centre for worship in Chinatown. (p66)

**Sri Mahamariamman Temple** The central Hindu temple in Chinatown. (p66)

**Sree Veera Hanuman Temple** Dedicated to the monkey king, the temple is flanked by two others. (p111)

**Masjid Negara** The national mosque was built in a striking modern design in 1965 to embody the postcolonial spirit. (p110)

**Thean Hou Temple** This gaudy modern Chinese temple has beautiful city views. (p119)

## Best Heritage Buildings

**Merdeka Square** Independence square is surrounded by beautiful colonial-era buildings. (p62)

**Old KL Train Station** This grand civic structure dates back to 1910. (p108)

**Rumah Penghulu Abu Seman** A gorgeous 100-year-old wood stilt house saved from Kedah state. (p48)

**Medan Pasar** KL's old market square is backed by beautiful shophouses with European-style facades. (p69)

**Loke Mansion** Built by tin tycoon Loke Yew, this is one of KL's most grand private mansions. (p86)

**Royal Museum** This sprawling European mansion was home to the Malay royal family until 2011. (p119)

# Best
# **Green Spaces**

LAURIE NOBLE/GETTY IMAGES ©

One of the pleasures of riding around KL in a taxi is suddenly coming round a bend into a stretch of intense greenery, often with towering banyan trees interweaving overhead that block out the sky. There are few small parks to relax in, but plenty of tree-lined roads and a number of larger lakes and forest parks both within the city and a short drive away.

### Wild Kuala Lumpur

Even in the city your chances of spotting exotic wildlife are high. Macaque monkeys are out in force at Batu Caves (do not touch or feed them, or other wildlife, as rabies is present in Malaysia). At FRIM or Taman TAR also look for adorable dusky leaf monkeys. If you have a vantage over the forest canopy, keep an eye out for brightly-coloured orioles and bee-eaters. Anytime you are near a body of water watch for monitor lizards (which can reach up to 2m in length). And if you really want to get into the mountains around town contact **KL Hiking & Trail Running** (www.facebook.com/groups/Wildpac).

### Best Parks & Lakes

**KLCC Park** This well-treed, 20-hectare park looks up to the Petronas Towers. (p43)

**Tun Abdul Razak Heritage Park** Formerly known as the Lake Gardens, it's the city's biggest green space. (p100)

**KL Forest Eco Park** KL's oldest protected jungle has a canopy walk and trails to/from Menara KL. (p45)

**Merdeka Square** A former cricket green, now an open square surrounded by colonial buildings. (p62)

**FRIM** Almost 600 hectares of forests and quiet lanes for cycling just outside the city. (p97)

**Batu Caves** Massive natural caves that you can walk into for almost 1km with a guide. (p95)

**Lake Titiwangsa** A pretty lake for strolling round and snapping KL's skyline. (p85)

**Kwong Tong Cemetery** Enjoy rolling hills and frangipani trees among the graves of Kuala Lumpur luminaries. (p119)

### Best Views

**Menara KL** Observe the ring of mountains around KL from this telcommunications tower. (p44)

**Petronas Towers** Offers another mesmerising panorama of the city. (p42)

Best
# Museums & Galleries

There are no world-class museums or galleries in KL, but the scene is rich nonetheless, with a high number of excellent small venues, and one or two outstanding collections in the larger museums. With the exception of the Islamic Arts Museum, all are focused on the details of Malaysian life, culture and history, or the creative works of native talents.

RICHARD CUMMINS/GETTY IMAGES ©

## Best for Arts & Crafts

**Islamic Arts Museum** KL's top museum sets out to display the variety and richness of Islamic art around the world. (p102)

**National Textiles Museum** In a beautiful heritage building, this museum charts the history of Malaysian textiles with lots of examples. (p63)

**Badan Warisan Malaysia** This heritage society holds exhibits in a colonial-era bungalow. (p48)

**Muzeum Kraf** Small but informative exhibits of traditional crafts such as wood carvings, metalwork and batik. (p48)

**Museum of Ethnic Arts** An outstanding private collection filled with tribal and ethnic arts, from Sarawak face masks to Qing-dynasty dragon robes. (p68)

## Best for History

**Royal Malaysia Police Museum** See homemade guns from Chinese triads and take in history of Malaysia through policing. (p101)

**National Museum** Excellent prehistory displays and an informative gallery on the early Malay Kingdoms. (p108)

**KL City Gallery** This is a great place to kick-start your understanding of Kuala Lumpur. (p63)

☑ **Top Tips**

▶ Most museums and galleries are free, or inexpensive, which is good because foreign student and senior discounts don't usually apply (though children's do).

▶ The galleries that are located in Publika mall (p37) are a good place to see (and purchase) contemporary oil paintings.

**Royal Museum** The former house of the royal family is now open for public viewing. (p104)

National Museum (p108)

## Best for Contemporary Art

**Bank Negara Malaysia Museum & Art Gallery** Though the painting collection is good, the floors devoted to money are better. (p84)

**National Visual Arts Gallery** Showcases the best of contemporary Malaysian artists working in a variety of media. (p85)

**Wei-Ling Gallery** One of the city's top private painting galleries is happy to welcome curious browsers. (p117)

**Galeri Petronas** This bright modern gallery owned by Petronas group showcases local and international painters and photographers. (p48)

## Worth a Trip

The family-friendly **National Science Centre** (Pusat Sains Negara; www.psn.gov.my; Persiaran Bukit Kiara; adult/child RM6/3; 9am-5pm Sat-Thu) in the Mont Kiara suburb is well regarded for its hands-on learning environment. The galleries cover topics such as flight, computers, water, air and light and the discoveries of Islamic scientists. There are also special rooms for toddlers and older kids, an outdoor park and a 3D theatre.

# Best
# **Spas & Wellness**

Like most Asian cities, KL has its share of dodgy massage places, but it also stands out for having some truly fine spas. And being such a multi-cultural city, you're as likely to find a Swedish massage joint as fish-nibbling foot spas, Moroccan-style bathhouses and Chinese *tuina* clinics where all your troubles can be kneaded away.

BTREKNEL/GETTY IMAGES ©

## Treatments

Spas offer a wide range of services, from a simple head and shoulder massage to a full package that includes skin scrubbing, steam baths and body wraps. Cheap foot and body massages can be found around Jln Alor, while most shopping malls will have a higher-end massage, spa and beauty clinic.

## Exercise

KL-ites are becoming more active these days, and gyms and yoga classes are easy to find, as are hiking, cycling and other outdoor activity clubs (look them up on Facebook or Meetup).

## Costs

Prices of treatments of course vary greatly, but a simple foot spa might start at RM40; a 60-minute massage at RM200; and a full spa treatment with massage, scrubs and wraps at RM400.

### Best Spas, Massages, Wellness & Fitness

**Hammam Spa** This gorgeous Moroccan-style spa and bathhouse offers exotic packages such as 'The Sultan's Daughter's Wedding'. (p121)

**Kenko** Renowned fish spa for when you need the grime of the city streets nibbled away. (p28)

**Donna Spa** A Balinese-style spa on the super-luxury Starhill Gallery's Pamper Floor. (p28)

**Eu Yan Sang** This traditional Chinese medicine clinic offers *tuina* massage, and scrapping therapies for heat exhaustion. (p39)

**Majestic Spa** Beautiful spa in one of KL's best heritage hotels. (p112)

**Buddhist Maha Vihara** Meditation classes at a Buddhist temple. (p110)

**Chin Woo Stadium** Old but good community fitness centre with big swimming pool. (p76)

# Survival Guide

**Before You Go**     **144**
When to Go . . . . . . . . . . . . . . . . . . . . . . . 144
Book Your Stay . . . . . . . . . . . . . . . . . . . . 144

**Arriving in Kuala Lumpur**     **145**

**Getting Around**     **146**
LRT, Monorail & Komuter Train . . . . . . 146
Taxi . . . . . . . . . . . . . . . . . . . . . . . . . . . . . . . 147
Tourist Buses . . . . . . . . . . . . . . . . . . . . . . 147

**Essential Information**     **148**
Business Hours . . . . . . . . . . . . . . . . . . . . 148
Discount Cards . . . . . . . . . . . . . . . . . . . . 148
Electricity . . . . . . . . . . . . . . . . . . . . . . . . . 148
Emergency . . . . . . . . . . . . . . . . . . . . . . . . 148
Money . . . . . . . . . . . . . . . . . . . . . . . . . . . . . 148
Public Holidays . . . . . . . . . . . . . . . . . . . . 149
Safe Travel . . . . . . . . . . . . . . . . . . . . . . . . 150
Telephone . . . . . . . . . . . . . . . . . . . . . . . . 150
Toilets . . . . . . . . . . . . . . . . . . . . . . . . . . . . 150
Tourist Information . . . . . . . . . . . . . . . . 150
Travellers with Disabilities . . . . . . . . . 150
Visas . . . . . . . . . . . . . . . . . . . . . . . . . . . . . . 151

**Language**     **152**

# Survival Guide

## Before You Go

### When to Go

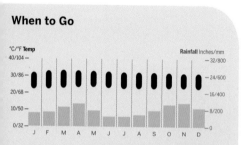

°C/°F Temp
40/104 —
30/86 —
20/68 —
10/50 —
0/32 —

Rainfall Inches/mm
— 32/800
— 24/600
— 16/400
— 8/200
— 0

J F M A M J J A S O N D

➡ **Dry Season (Jan–Feb)**
Generally dry with hot days and cooler nights. Busy tourist season with Chinese New Year and Hindu Thaipusam festival.

➡ **Wet Season (Mar–May)** Expect heavy afternoon monsoon showers and slow traffic.

➡ **Dry Season (Jun–Sep)**
Driest and hottest time of year and most tourist-ed. Especially popular with Middle Eastern travellers July and August. Enjoy fresh durians June to August and Ramadan feasts in August.

➡ **Wet Season (Oct–Dec)**
Another rainy season with heavy afternoon showers. Tourist numbers lower and nights are pleasant.

## Book Your Stay
☑ **Top Tip** If you're planning to stay in a hostel, check that it doesn't have an age limit policy that might restrict you: some hostels refuse guests over 60 or 65, or under 13.

KL has plenty of good accommodation, more and more of it set in colonial-era buildings, at all price ranges. It's always best to reserve in advance, especially around Chinese New Year, the summer months (especially Ramadan) and holidays such as Deepavali. Rates at cheaper places usually include hotel taxes (which are currently 6% but could change with the implementation of a GST in 2015) and service charges (10%). Midrange and top-end places usually quote prices without these added.

### Useful Websites

**Lonely Planet** (www.lonely planet.com) Read reviews and make bookings.

**Agoda** (www.agoda.com) Big discounts on hotel rates.

**iBilik** (www.ibilik.my) Short-term rental apartments and homestays.

**Cari Homestay** (www.carihomestay.net) More homestay options.

### Best Budget

**Reggae Mansion** (www.reggaehostelsmalaysia.com/mansion) In Chinatown; for the modern, chilled-out backpacker.

**Classic Inn** (www.classicinn.com.my) Retro-charming shophouse near the Imbi monorail.

**Red Palm** (www.redpalm-kl.com) Shophouse hostel in the heart of KL's eating and drinking scene.

**BackHome** (www.backhome.com.my) Relaxed Chinatown hostel aimed at the flashpacker set.

**Explorers Guesthouse** (www.theexplorersguesthouse.com) Well run, a little arty, and in the heart of Chinatown.

### Best Midrange

**Paloma Inn** (www.hotelpalomainn.com.my) Cosy digs on a quiet backstreet of painted shophouses.

**Sarang Vacation Homes** (www.sarangvacationhomes.com) Friendly B&B operation with a variety of flats and shophouses.

**Yard Boutique Hotel** (www.theyard.com.my) Stylish oasis in a buzzing bar and restaurant district.

**Rainforest Bed & Breakfast** (www.rainforestbnbhotel.com) Colourful, timber-lined guesthouse on hipster Jln Mesui.

### Best Top End

**Sekeping Sin Chew Kee** (www.sekeping.com) Architect-designed family apartment in a renovated shophouse.

**Royale Chulan** (www.theroyalechulan.com.my) Luxe hotel in a leafy neighbourhood just minutes from KLCC.

**Majestic Hotel** (www.majestickl.com) Reborn heritage hotel within walking distance of the Lake Gardens.

**Villa Samadhi** (www.villasamadhi.com.my) Beautiful Southeast Asian–style hideaway with a tree-shaded pool.

# Arriving in Kuala Lumpur

☑ **Top Tip** For the best way to get to your accommodation, see p17.

## Kuala Lumpur International Airport

➜ Unless you're coming in by bus or train from Penang, Malacca, Thailand or Singapore, you will arrive at **Kuala Lumpur International Airport** (KLIA; ☎ 03-8777 8888; www.klia.com.my), about 50km south of the city centre. Note that after the low-cost terminal (LCCT) closed in 2014, all flights now arrive at this airport. There are two terminals: KLIA I and II, the latter the new low-cost-carrier terminal.

➜ The airport is connected with the city centre by taxi, bus and train. The fastest way is by **KLIA Ekspres** (www.kliaekspres.com; adult/child one-way RM35/15) trains, which take 28 to 33 minutes and have departures every 15 to 20 minutes from 5am to 1am to KL Sentral station.

→ An **airport express bus** (www.airportcoach.com.my) also runs between KLIA and KL Sentral station from 5am to midnight. The fare is a low RM10.

→ A taxi costs RM75 to RM100; prepay for your ride before exiting the arrival hall.

→ There are ATMs, moneychangers and left-luggage services at both terminals.

## KL Sentral Train Station

All long-distance train services arrive at **KL Sentral station** (☎1300 889 933; www.ktmb.com.my) of the **KTM** (Keretapi Tanah Melayu Berhad; www.ktmkomuter.com.my) national railway hub and near the heart of the city in Brickfields. There are daily connections with Butterworth (for Penang), Thailand and Singapore but the journey times can be very slow.

KL Sentral is linked to all major local public transport networks: LRT, monorail, Komuter trains and buses. Taxis are also available; purchase a taxi coupon (there are booths on various levels) before lining up to ensure

you are not overcharged. Level 2 is open from 6am to 2pm.

## Terminal Bersepadu Selatan

The slick **transport hub** (TBS; www.tbsbts.com.my) is situated about 15 minutes south of KL Sentral and connected by train; LRT (Bandar Tasik Selatan station); and taxi. Buses from north and south destinations within Malaysia arrive here, as well as from Singapore.

## Pudu Sentral Bus Station

This **bus station** (www.expressbusmalaysia.com/bus-stations/puduraya-bus-terminal; Jln Pudu) on the edge of Chinatown serves northbound destinations around Peninsular Malaysia, as well as Thailand. It's a crowded, rundown place, with pushy touts, and best avoided if other options are available. Plaza Rakyat LRT station is just behind the terminal. Taking a taxi to or from this station will always be a hassle.

# Getting Around

## LRT, Monorail & Komuter Train

☑ **Best for...** Getting around the city quickly to most tourist spots, especially when it rains and traffic comes to a standstill.

→ It's best to think of the three systems as forming one mass transport network (and this is how most maps will show them) across greater KL; they share a main hub at KL Sentral and you can transfer from one to the other (though they are not well integrated).

→ The air-conditioned **KL Monorail** (www.klmonorail.com.my; RM1.20-2.50; ◷6am-midnight) has a single line from KL Sentral to Titiwangsa, cutting through the Golden Triangle and linking together most of the tourist sights in the city. Trains run every six to 12 minutes. The line gets very busy in the evening and can be a little unsettling when it wobbles.

→ The **LRT** (Light Rapid Transit; ☎03-7885 2585; www.myrapid.com.my;

RM1-2.80; ⏰6am-11.45pm) covers much more of the city centre and the outer suburbs, with lines that take you to Chinatown and Masjid Jamek, as well as Bangsar and Ampang. Runs every six to 10 minutes.

➜ The **KTM Komuter Train** (www.ktmkomuter.com. my; RM1.40; ⏰6.45am-11.45pm) runs every 15 to 20 minutes serving greater KL and is useful for trips to Batu Caves, FRIM and the Lake Gardens.

## Taxi

☑ **Best for...** Travel to and from hotels and restaurants, travelling quickly between destinations during non-peak, non-rainy hours.

➜ Air-conditioned taxis are plentiful in KL and you can usually flag one down easily during non-peak, non-rainy hours.

➜ Regular taxis charge RM3 for first kilometre and 87 sen for each additional kilometre. There's a 50% surcharge from midnight to 6am. Luggage placed in the trunk is charged extra at RM1 per piece.

➜ Blue taxis are newer and more comfortable,

and start at RM6 for the first 2km and RM1 per kilometre after that. Night surcharges of 50% also apply.

➜ There is a serious problem in KL with drivers refusing to use meters (even though they are required to do so by law) and overcharging tourists by up to three times the normal fare. Never use an unmarked taxi or get into any taxi if the driver looks drunk. If possible, use a taxi booking smartphone app such as My Teksi, which records the entire ride's GPS data, as well as the driver's name, license plate number, and the fact you booked it. MyTeksi drivers have to use the meter (and the service lets you know before you book approximately how much it will cost).

➜ Most shopping malls, as well as KL Sentral, have taxi booths where you either prepay for your ride (letting the cashier know where you want to go), or pay RM2 for a voucher which guarantees the driver will use his meter.

## Tourist Buses

☑ **Best for...** Getting around to the sights. Avoid KL's slow public buses.

➜ The double-decker, wi-fi enabled buses of the **KL Hop-On Hop-Off** (☎2166 6162; www.myhoponhopoff. com; adult/child 24hr RM45/24, 48hr RM79/43; ⏰9am-8pm) program stop at 42 sights and attractions (including major shopping malls and 100 hotels). Buses run every 30 minutes, though between 4pm and 6pm you may have to wait for one with seats. Stops are

## Tickets & Passes

➜ Rapid KL offers the **MyRapid** (www.myrapid.com. my) pre-paid card, valid on RapidKL buses, the monorail and the main LRT lines.

➜ **Touch 'n Go** (www.touchngo.com.my) cards can be used on all public transport.

➜ For short-term stays you are better off buying individual tickets, as finding an outlet or station stocked with these cards can be difficult.

obvious and you can, as the name suggests, get on and off at will, with a single ticket. Tickets are valid for 24 or 48 hours from your first ride. You can purchase online or directly on the bus.

➡ **Go KL City Bus** is a free bus service that is run by **Rapid KL** (www.myrapid.com.my). It's good for getting around the city between neighbourhoods.

# Essential Information

## Business Hours

**Banks** 10am to 3pm Monday to Friday, 9.30am to 11.30am Saturday.

**Restaurants** Noon to 2.30pm and 6pm to 10.30pm.

**Shops** 9.30am to 7pm, malls 10am to 10pm, usually closed either Monday or Tuesday.

**Bars** 5pm to 1am Sunday to Thursday, to 3am Friday and Saturday.

**Clubs** 9pm to 3am Tuesday or Wednesday to Saturday.

## Discount Cards

Some top-end shopping malls offer select discounts if you register with your passport at the information desk.

## Electricity

240V/50Hz

## Emergency

**Fire** ☏994

**Police & Ambulance** ☏999 (also ☏112 from cell phone)

**Tourist Police** ☏2166 8322

## Money

The basic unit of Malaysian money is the ringgit (RM), which is comprised of 100 sens. Coins in use are 1 sen, 5 sen, 10 sen, 20 sen and 50 sen; notes are RM1, RM5, RM10, RM50 and RM100.

### ATMs

Most banks and shopping malls provide international ATMs linked to international banking networks such as Cirrus, Maestro and Plus. Your best bet are Maybank and HSBC ATMs, but note it's common for cards not to be accepted in some ATM machines, or for your daily limit to be less than at home. Ideally bring two cards with you and some cash (or even travellers cheques). Also check with your home bank about its reciprocal relationships with Malaysian banks.

### Credit Cards

➡ Credit cards are widely accepted, though at small shops and restaurants it's usually cash only. Visa followed by MasterCard and AMEX are the most widely accepted credit cards.

➡ Cash advances on credit cards at major banks are possible.

**Tipping**

➡ In better restaurants expect a 10% service fee. In casual places locals often leave the change after paying.

➡ Tip taxi drivers who help with your bags, porters in hotels (couple of RM per bag) and housekeeping (couple of RM per day).

**Travellers Cheques & Cash**

➡ Malaysian banks will exchange cash and travellers cheques and there are plenty of moneychangers about. Banks usually charge a commission for cashing cheques (around RM10 per transaction, with a possible extra fee for each cheque), whereas moneychangers have no charges but their rates are more variable.

➡ All major brands of travellers cheques are accepted. Cash in major currencies is also readily exchanged, though the US dollar has a slight edge.

**Taxes**

A GST (goods and services tax) of 6% will be implemented in April 2015. The 10% service fee added to meals, hotel rooms and other services at midrange to top-end places is likely to remain. This fee (which is not a tax) is often expressed as '++' next to the price. Tourists are expected to be able to apply for a GST refund on goods taken out of the country.

**Public Holidays**

As well as fixed secular holidays, various religious festivals (which change dates annually) are national holidays. These include Chinese New Year (January/

February), the Hindu festival of Deepavali (October/November), the Buddhist festival of Wesak (April/May) and the Muslim festivals of Hari Raya Haji, Hari Raya Puasa, Mawlid al-Nabi and Awal Muharram (Muslim New Year).

Fixed annual holidays include the following:

**New Year's Day** 1 January

**Federal Territory Day** 1 February

**Labor Day** 1 May

**Yang di-Pertuan Agong's (Kings) Birthday** 1st Saturday in June

**National Day** (Hari Kebang-saan) 31 August

**Christmas Day** 25 December

### Managing Kuala Lumpur's Many Holidays

Malaysia has a full roster of public holidays and during Ramadan, Deepavali and Chinese New Year there is a festive atmosphere about town, much like Christmas in the West. Be aware that hotels and transport can be booked solid, and restaurants, banks, museums and other tourist attractions closed during these times. ATMs may also be short on cash (before Ramadan is particularly bad for withdrawals). The city never entirely shuts down, and when one ethnic group is off celebrating, another will usually take the slack. During Chinese New Year, for example, many Chinese go to Little India to eat.

## Safe Travel

KL is generally safe, but there are a lot of seedy areas in the city, violent attacks in popular nightlife areas are not infrequent, and scams and even assaults by taxi drivers are far too common. So keep your wits about you.

Watch for pickpockets and see p147 for advice on safe travel by taxi. Bathrooms in malls are often very isolated so never send children there alone.

### Dengue Fever

An extremely serious threat in recent years. Cover up exposed skin and wear a strong mosquito repellent.

### Scams

The most common scams involve seemingly friendly locals. Anyone who accosts you in the street asking where you come from or claiming to have a 'relative studying abroad' may be setting you up for a scam – the best tactic is not to reply at all.

Use credit cards only at established businesses and guard card numbers closely.

### Theft & Violence

Bag snatches are common and muggings are becoming more frequent. Keep bags close to your side, and be aware of any motorcycles approaching you from behind.

## Telephone

### Mobile Phones

➡ Malaysia is on a GSM and 3G/4G network. You can pick up a local SIM card at the airport on arrival from one of three local carriers: **Celcom** (www.celcom.com.my); **DiGi** (www.digi.com.my); or **Maxis** (www.maxis.com.my). A five-day plan with 16 minutes of local calls and 2G of data costs around RM28. To top up your credit look for a phone shop in any mall.

➡ For international calls your first choice should be to use a VOIP service app or laptop software such as Skype, which works on wi-fi or 3G.

### Useful Numbers

➡ Malaysia country code: ☎60

➡ Kuala Lumpur city code: ☎03 (you must use this prefix when calling a landline from a mobile phone)

➡ International access code from Malaysia: ☎00

➡ Operator-assisted calls: ☎101

## Toilets

Western-style sit-down toilets are becoming the norm, but squat toilets are still common. Toilet paper is not usually provided. Public toilets in malls often charge entry, which usually includes toilet paper. Cleanliness is generally tolerable to quite good.

## Tourist Information

**Visit KL** (Map p64; A3; ☎2698 0332; www.visitkl.gov.my; KL City Gallery, Merdeka Sq; ⊙9am-6.30pm; 🗢; 🚇Masjid Jamek) The official city tourism office has helpful staff, informative displays and a great city tourist map.

## Travellers with Disabilities

For the mobility impaired, KL can be a nightmare. There are often no footpaths, kerbs can be very high, construction sites are everywhere, and pedestrian crossings are few and far between.

Before setting off get in touch with your national support organisation. Also try the following:

**Accessible Journeys** (www.disabilitytravel.com) In the US.

**Mobility International USA** (www.miusa.org) In the US.

**Nican** (www.nican.com.au) In Australia.

**Tourism For All** (www.tourismforall.org.uk) In the UK.

## Visas

➡ Visitors must have a passport valid for at least six months beyond the date of entry, and may need proof of an onward ticket and sufficient funds. The rules for visa and visa-on-arrival entries are ever changing for some countries; see https:// malaysia.visahq.com for guidelines.

➡ In general, travellers from Western nations, Japan and many Middle Eastern countries receive a stamp on arrival for a 90-day stay. Nationals from Singapore, the Netherlands, Switzerland and Russia receive 30 days. Most other nationals require pre-arranged visas.

# Language

The official language of Kuala Lumpur is Malay, or Bahasa Malaysia, as it's called by its speakers. It is very similar to Indonesian.

Malay pronunciation is easy to master. Each letter always represents the same sound and most letters are pronounced the same as their English counterparts, with c pronounced as the 'ch' in 'chat' and sy as the 'sh' in 'ship'. Note also that kh is a guttural sound (like the 'ch' in the Scottish loch), and that gh is a throaty 'g' sound.

To enhance your trip with a phrasebook, visit **lonelyplanet.com**. Lonely Planet iPhone phrasebooks are available through the Apple App store.

## Basics

| | |
|---|---|
| **Hello.** | Helo. |
| **Goodbye.** | |
| (by person leaving) | Selamat tinggal. |
| (by person staying) | Selamat jalan. |
| **Yes.** | Ya. |
| **No.** | Tidak. |
| **Please.** | Tolong. |
| **Thank you.** | Terima kasih. |
| **You're welcome.** | Sama-sama. |
| **Excuse me.** | Maaf. |
| **Sorry.** | Minta maaf. |
| **How are you?** | Apa khabar? |
| **Fine, thanks.** | Khabar baik. |

**Do you speak English?**
Bolehkah anda berbicara Bahasa Inggeris?

**I don't understand.**
Saya tidak faham.

## Eating & Drinking

**Can I see the menu?**
Minta senarai makanan?

**I'd like ...**      Saya mahu...

**I'm a vegetarian.**
Saya makan sayur-sayuran sahaja.

**Not too spicy, please.**
Kurang pedas.

**Please add extra chilli.**
Tolong letak cili lebih.

**Thank you, that was delicious.**
Sedap sekali, terima kasih.

**Please bring the bill.**
Tolong bawa bil.

## Shopping

| | |
|---|---|
| **I'd like to buy ...** | Saya nak beli ... |
| **I'm just looking.** | Saya nak tengok saja. |

**Can I look at it?**
Boleh saya lihat barang itu?

| | |
|---|---|
| **I don't like it.** | Saya tak suka ini. |
| **How much is it?** | Berapa harganya? |
| **It's too expensive.** | Mahalnya. |

**Can you lower the price?**
Boleh kurang sedikit?

## Emergencies

| | |
|---|---|
| **Help!** | Tolong! |
| **Go away!** | Pergi! |
| **I'm lost.** | Saya sesat. |

**There's been an accident.**
Ada kemalangan.

| | |
|---|---|
| **Call a doctor!** | Panggil doktor! |
| **Call the police!** | Panggil polis! |

| | |
|---|---|
| **I'm ill.** | *Saya sakit.* |
| **It hurts here.** | *Sini sakit.* |
| **I'm allergic to (antibiotics).** | |
| *Saya alergik kepada (antibiotik).* | |
| **Tandas** | Toilets |

## Time & Numbers

| | |
|---|---|
| **What time is it?** | *Pukul berapa?* |
| **It's (seven) o'clock.** | *Pukul (tujuh).* |
| **Half past (one).** | *Pukul (satu) setengah.* |
| **in the morning** | *pagi* |
| **in the afternoon** | *tengahari* |
| **in the evening** | *petang* |
| **yesterday** | *semalam* |
| **today** | *hari ini* |
| **tomorrow** | *esok* |
| **Monday** | *hari Isnin* |
| **Tuesday** | *hari Selasa* |
| **Wednesday** | *hari Rabu* |
| **Thursday** | *hari Khamis* |
| **Friday** | *hari Jumaat* |
| **Saturday** | *hari Sabtu* |
| **Sunday** | *hari Minggu* |
| **1** | *satu* |
| **2** | *dua* |
| **3** | *tiga* |
| **4** | *empat* |
| **5** | *lima* |
| **6** | *enam* |
| **7** | *tujuh* |
| **8** | *lapan* |
| **9** | *sembilan* |
| **10** | *sepuluh* |
| **20** | *dua puluh* |
| **30** | *tiga puluh* |
| **40** | *empat puluh* |
| **50** | *lima puluh* |
| **60** | *enam puluh* |
| **70** | *tujuh puluh* |
| **80** | *lapan puluh* |
| **90** | *sembilan puluh* |
| **100** | *seratus* |
| **1000** | *seribu* |

## Transport & Directions

| | |
|---|---|
| **I want to go to ...** | *Saya nak ke ...* |
| **What time does the (bus) leave?** | |
| *(Bas) bertolak pukul berapa?* | |
| **What time does the (train) arrive?** | |
| *(Keretapi) tiba pukul berapa?* | |
| **Can you tell me when we get to ...?** | |
| *Tolong beritahu saya bila kita sudah sampai di ...?* | |
| **I want to get off at ...** | |
| *Saya nak turun di ...* | |
| **bicycle-rickshaw** | *beca* |
| **boat** | *bot* |
| **bus** | *bas* |
| **plane** | *kapal terbang* |
| **ship** | *kapal* |
| **taxi** | *teksi* |
| **train** | *keretapi* |
| **Where is ...?** | *Di mana ...?* |
| **What's the address?** | *Apakah alamatnya?* |
| **Can you write the address, please?** | |
| *Tolong tuliskan alamat itu?* | |
| **Can you show me (on the map)?** | |
| *Tolong tunjukkan (di peta)?* | |
| **Go straight ahead.** | *Jalan terus.* |
| **Turn left.** | *Belok kiri.* |
| **Turn right.** | *Belok kanan.* |

# Behind the Scenes

## Send Us Your Feedback

We love to hear from travellers – your comments help make our books better. We read every word, and we guarantee that your feedback goes straight to the authors. Visit **lonelyplanet.com/contact** to submit your updates and suggestions.

Note: We may edit, reproduce and incorporate your comments in Lonely Planet products such as guidebooks, websites and digital products, so let us know if you don't want your comments reproduced or your name acknowledged. For a copy of our privacy policy visit lonelyplanet.com/privacy.

## Robert's Thanks

Thanks to Hardeep, local fount of knowledge. To Mauro and company, I appreciate you letting me test out itineraries on you. But most importantly, I dedicate this first edition of *Pocket Kuala Lumpur* to my soon-to-be wife Tania Simonetti, and our soon-to-be child, as yet un-named but very much loved.

## Acknowledgments

Cover photograph: Petronas Towers and KLCC, Maurizio Rellini/4Corners.

## This Book

This 1st edition of *Pocket Kuala Lumpur* was researched and written by Robert Kelly. The guidebook was produced by the following:

**Destination Editor** Sarah Reid **Product Editors** Katie O'Connell, Alison Ridgway **Regional Senior Cartographer** Julie Sheridan **Book Designer** Virginia Moreno **Assisting Editors** Andrea Dobbin, Gabrielle Stefanos **Cover Researcher** Naomi Parker **Thanks to** Elizabeth Jones, Kate Mathews, Claire Naylor, Karyn Noble, Luna Soo, Lauren Wellicome, Tony Wheeler

# Index

See also separate subindexes for:

⊗ **Eating p157**
⊝ **Drinking p158**
☆ **Entertainment p158**
⊕ **Shopping p158**

**A**
accommodation 144-5
airports 145-6
Ampang 92-3, **92**
**Aquaria KLCC 43**
architecture 50, 70, 138
area codes 150
art galleries 140-1
ATMs 148

**B**
**Badan Warisan Malaysia 48**
Bangsar Baru 120-1, **120**
**Bank Negara Malaysia Museum & Art Gallery 84**
bathrooms 150
**Batu Caves 10, 94-5**
bicycle travel 69, 97
**Bird Park 101**
Brickfields 98-117, **106-7**
  drinking 115-16
  entertainment 116
  food 112-15
  itineraries 99
  shopping 117
  sights 100-5, 108-12
  transport 99

**Sights 000**
Map Pages **000**

**Brickfields Heritage Walk 109**
**Buddhist Maha Vihara 110**
budgeting 16, 148
bus travel 146, 147-8
business hours 148
**Butterfly Park 109-10**

**C**
cell phones 16, 150
**Central Market 67-8**
**Chan She Shu Yuen Clan Association Temple 66**
**Chetty Street (Lebuh Ampang) 68**
children, travel with 134
Chinatown 60-79, **64-5**
  drinking 74-6
  entertainment 76-7
  food 69-73
  itineraries 61
  shopping 78-9
  sights 62-3, 66-9
  transport 61
  walks 126-7, **127**
Chow Kit 80-91, **82-3**
  entertainment 91
  food 88-91
  itineraries 81
  sights 84-8
  transport 81
**City Gallery 63**
climate 144

clubs 136-7, see also Entertainment subindex
coffee 35
costs 148
credit cards 148
currency 16
cycling 69, 97

**D**
dangers 150
**Dark Cave 95**
**Dataran Merdeka Heritage Walk 67**
dengue fever 150
disabilities, travellers with 150-1
**Donna Spa 28-9**
drinking 130-1, see also individual neighbourhoods, Drinking subindex

**E**
electricity 16, 148
emergencies 148
entertainment 136-7, see also individual neighbourhoods, Entertainment subindex

**F**
food 32, 128-9, see also individual neighbourhoods, Eating subindex

**Forestry Research Institute of Malaysia (FRIM) 11, 96-7**
free attractions 135

**G**
**Galeri Petronas 48-9**
galleries 140-1
gardens 139
gay travellers 55
Golden Triangle 22-37, **26-7**
  drinking 31-5
  entertainment 35
  food 29-31
  itineraries 23, 24-5, **24**
  shopping 36-7
  sights 28-9
  transport 23
**Guandi Temple 68**

**H**
Hammam Spa 121
health 15
heritage buildings 138
highlights 12-13
hiking 97
holidays 149
**Hundred Quarters 109**

**I**
Islam 114
**Islamic Arts Museum 10, 102-3**

itineraries 14-15, 124-7, **125**, **127**, *see also individual neighbourhoods*

**J**
Jalan Ampang Hilir 93
Jalan Dagang 93
Jalan U-Thant 93

**K**
Kampung Baru 80-91, **82-3**
entertainment 91
food 88-91
itineraries 81
sights 84-8
transport 81
walks 84, 124-5, **125**
**Kampung Baru Walking Tour 84**
**Kenko 28**
KL Academy of Traditional Chinese Medicine 78
**KL Bird Park 101**
**KL Butterfly Park 109-10**
**KL City Gallery 63**
KLCC 40-59, **46-7**
drinking 53-6
entertainment 56-8
food 50-3
itineraries 41
shopping 58-9
sights 42-5, 48-50
transport 41
**KLCC Park 43**
**KTM Headquarters Building 108**

**Kwong Tong Cemetery 105**

**L**
Lake Gardens 98-117, **106-7**
drinking 115-16
entertainment 116
food 112-15
itineraries 99
shopping 117
sights 100-5, 108-12
transport 117
**Lake Titiwangsa 85**
language 16, 58, 152-3
**Lebuh Ampang (Chetty Street) 68**
lesbian travellers 55
lightning 117
Little India 115
live music 136, *see also Entertainment subindex*
local life 12-13
**Loke Mansion 86, 88**

**M**
**Majestic Spa 112**
**Malay World Ethnology Museum 108**
malls 37
**Masjid India 88**
Masjid India area 80-91, **82-3**
entertainment 91
food 88-91
itineraries 81
sights 84-8
transport 81
**Masjid Jamek 66-7**
**Masjid Jamek Kampung Baru 86**
**Masjid Negara 110**
massages 142
**Medan Pasar 69**

**Menara KL 10, 44-5**
**Merdeka Square 9, 62-3**
Merdeka Square area 60-79, **64-5**
drinking 74-6
entertainment 76-7
food 69-73
itineraries 61
shopping 78-9
sights 62-3, 66-9
transport 61
mobile phones 16, 150
money 16, 148-9
mosques 138
multiculturalism 57
**Museum of Ethnic Arts 68**
museums 140-1
**Muslim Cemetery 50**
**Muzeum Kraf 48**

**N**
**National Museum 108**
**National Science Centre 141**
**National Textiles Museum 63**
**National Visual Arts Gallery 85**

**O**
**Old High Court Building 68**
**Old KL Train Station 108**
opening hours 148
**Orang Asli Craft Museum 108**

**P**
parks 139
**Perdana Botanical Garden 101**
**Petronas Towers 8, 42-3**

Petronas Towers area 40-59, **46-7**
drinking 53-6
entertainment 56-8
food 50-3
itineraries 41
shopping 58-9
sights 42-5, 48-50
transport 41
**Petrosains 49**
public holidays 149
Pudu 38-9, **38**
Pusaka 90

**R**
Ramadan 86
**Ramayana Cave 95**
religious buildings 138
**Royal Malaysia Police Museum 101**
**Royal Museum 11, 104-5**
**Royal Selangor Club 63**
**Rumah Penghulu Abu Seman 48**

**S**
safe travel 150
**Sam Kow Tong Temple 111**
scams 150
shopping 37, 132-3, *see also individual neighbourhoods, Shopping subindex*
**Sin Sze Si Ya Temple 66**
spas 142
**Sree Veera Hanuman Temple 111**
**Sri Kandaswamy Temple 110**
**Sri Mahamariamman Temple 66**
**Sri Sakthi Vinayagar Temple 108**

Sights p000
Map Pages p000

St John's Cathedral 69
St Mary's Anglican
    Cathedral 68-9
Stadium Merdeka 69
Starhill Culinary
    Studio 28
Sultan Abdul Samad
    Building 63
Sultan Sulaiman
    Club 86

**T**

Tabung Haji 49
Taman TAR 93
Taman Tasik 93
Tatt Khalsa Diwan
    Gurdwara 86
taxes 149
taxis 147
telephone services
    150
Temple Cave 95
temples 138
Thean Hou Temple 11,
    118-19
theft 150
time 16
tipping 16, 149
toilets 150
tourist information
    150
train travel 146-7
transport 17, 145-8
travellers cheques 149
Tun Abdul Razak
    Heritage Park 9,
    100-1

**V**

vacations 149
views 139
visas 16, 151
Vivekananda Ashram
    110

**W**

walks 124-7, **125**, **127**
weather 144
websites 16, 144-5

**Y**

Yap Ah Loy 75

**⊗ Eating**

**A**

ABC Stall 115
Al-Amar Express 25
Al-Amar Lebanese
    Cuisine 30
Annalakshmi Vegetarian
    Restaurant 112
Atmosphere 360 52

**B**

Bazaar Baru Chow
    Kit 88
Bijan 30
Brickfields Pisang
    Goreng 115

**C**

Capital Café 89
Chee Cheong Fun Stall 72
Coliseum Cafe 90
Colonial Cafe 115
Cuisine Gourmet by
    Nathalie 52

**D**

Devi's Corner 121
Dharma Realm Guan
    Yin Sagely Monastery
    Canteen 51
Din Tai Fung 30
D'Istana Jalamas
    Café 88

**F**

Feeka Coffee
    Roasters 29
Fierce Curry House 115
Frangipani 31

**G**

G3 Kitchen & Bar 121
Green Tomato Cafe 93

**H**

Hakka 29
Hon Kee 25, 73
Hong Ngek 69, 71
Hornbill Restaurant 113

**I**

Ikan Bakar Berempah 90
Ikan Bakar Jalan
    Bellamy 105
Imbi Market 24
Islamic Arts Museum
    restaurant 103

**J**

Jalan Alor 25
Jalan Melati 25
Jalan Utara 25
Jassal Tandoori
    Restaurant 113

**K**

Kak Som 89
Kedai Makanan Dan
    Minuman TKS 30
Kim Lian Kee 25, 71
Kin Kin 88
Kompleks Makan
    Tanglin 112
Kong Tai 25

**L**

La Vie En Rose 52
Lian Bee 72

Lima Blas 29
Little India Fountain
    Hawker Stalls 115
Little Penang Kafé 51
Living Food 51
LOKL 73
Lot 10 Hutong 25

**M**

Madras Lane Hawkers 72
Masjid India Hawker
    Court 89
Melur & Thyme 51
Mungo Jerry 90

**N**

Nasi Kandar Pelita 50
Nerovivo 31
Ngau Kee 25

**O**

Old China Café 72

**P**

Pasar Malam 88
Peter Hoe Beyond
    Cafe 73
Precious Old China 73

**R**

Rani Vilas Restoran 95
Restoran Santa 72
Restoran Win Heng
    Seng 25
Restoran Yusoof dan
    Zakhir 71
RGB & the Bean Hive 51

**S**

Santouka 29
Sao Nam 29-30
Saravanaa Bhavan 91
Sisters Crispy Popiah
    24

Soong Kee 25
Sri Nirwana Maju 121

**T**

Tamarind Springs 93
Teluk Intan Chee
    Cheung Fu 24
Tengkat Tong Shin 25
Troika Sky Dining 53

**V**

Vishal 112

**W**

Wong Ah Wah 30
Woods Macrobiotics 30

**Y**

Yut Kee 90

**Z**

Zaini Satay 93

🍸 **Drinking**

**A**

Ah Weng Koh Hainan
    Tea 24
Aku Cafe & Gallery 74
Albion KL 34
Apartment Downtown 54

**B**

Blueboy Discotheque
    34

**C**

Changkat Bukit Bintang
    25

Coffee Stain 36

**D**

Drawing Room 116

**F**

Frangipani 31
Fuego 53

**G**

Green Man 34

**H**

Heli Lounge Bar 54
Hit & Mrs 131

**J**

Jalan Mesui 25

**K**

Koong Woh Tong 76
Kuala Lumpur Pub
    Crawl 34

**L**

Luk Yu Tea House 34-5
Luna Bar 54

**M**

MAI Bar 115
Marini's on 57 54-5
Moontree House 74, 76

**N**

Neo Tamarind 55

**O**

Omakase +
    Appreciate 74

**P**

Pisco Bar 31

**R**

Reggae Bar 74

Reggae Mansion 74
Ril's Bangsar 121

**S**

Sky Bar 54
Social 121
Starhill Tea Salon 34

**T**

Taps Beer Bar 31, 33
Tate 55
Tea Lounge 116

**V**

Village Bar 33

**W**

Whisky Bar Kuala
    Lumpur 33

**Z**

Zouk 55-6

🎭 **Entertainment**

Chin Woo Stadium 76
Coliseum Theatre 91
Dewan Filharmonik
    Petronas 56
GSC Pavilion KL 35
Istana Budaya 91
Kelantan Shadow
    Puppet Play 76
KL Live 56
Kuala Lumpur Performing
    Arts Centre 137
Muzium Musik 77
No Black Tie 35
Panggung Bandaraya 76
Petaling Street Art
    House 77
Sutra Dance Theatre 91
Temple of Fine Arts 116
TGV Cineplex 56

Time Out Comedy
    Thursday 56

🛍 **Shopping**

Alexis Ampang 93
Ang Eng 58, 93
Aseana 59
Bangsar Village I & II 121
Central Market 78
Desiree 121
Dude & the Duchess 121
Fahrenheit88 36-7
Great Eastern Mall 93
House of Rinpo 78
Junk Bookstore 78
Khoon Hooi 37
Kompleks Kraf Kuala
    Lumpur 58
Kwong Yik Seng 79
Lavanya Arts 117
My Batik 93
Never Follow Suit 121
Nu Sentral 117
Nurita Harith 121
Pavilion KL 36
Petaling Street Market 79
Peter Hoe Beyond 78
Plaza Low Yat 37
Purple Cane Tea Arts 79
Royal Selangor 36
Royal Selangor Visitor
    Centre 133
Sang Kee 79
Semua House Wedding
    Shop 91
Shoes Shoes Shoes 121
Silverfish Books 121
Sonali 117
Starhill Gallery 36
Suria KLCC 59
Tenmoku Pottery 59
Thomas Chan 93, 121
Wei-Ling Gallery 117

# Our Writer

### Robert Kelly

A frequent visitor to KL, Robert finally settled in the city in 2013, moving into the jungly hills east of the city centre where he wrote this guide. Having lived in Taiwan for 15 years prior, Robert enjoys the familiarity of Chinatown, just one element of the enchanting KL *mise-en-scène* – a gloriously diverse stage of food, languages, styles and peoples. The freelance writer and photographer has also contributed to Lonely Planet guides to Taiwan, China, Alaska and Tibet, and is currently working on a collection of travel stories set in Asia which will feature a history of coffee drinking in Malaysia.

**Published by Lonely Planet Publications Pty Ltd**
ABN 36 005 607 983
1st edition – June 2015
ISBN 978 1 74360 514 1
© Lonely Planet 2015   Photographs © as indicated 2015
10 9 8 7 6 5 4 3 2 1
Printed in China